ALTERNATIVE CAREERS IN SECRET OPERATIONS

Your Guide to a New Identity, New Life, New Career

Mark W. Merritt

IMPACT PUBLICATIONS
Manassas Park, VA

Alternative Careers In Secret Operations

Copyright © 1998 by Mark W. Merritt

Library of Congress Cataloging-in-Publication Data

Merritt, Mark W
    Alternative careers in secret operations : your guide to a new identity, new life, new career / Mark W. Merritt.
       p. cm.
    ISBN 1-57023-092-7 (alk. paper)
    1. Intelligence service—Vocational guidance—United States.
    2. Business intelligence—Vocational guidance—United States.
    I. Title.
JK468.I6M47   1998   97-51732
327.12'023'73—dc21   CIP

For information on quantity discounts, please call (703/361-7300), fax (703/335-9486), or write to: Sales Department, Impact Publications, 9104-N Manassas Drive, Manassas Park, VA 20111-5211. Distributed to the trade by National Book Network, 15200 NBN Way, Blue Ridge Summit, PA 17214, Tel. 1-800-462-6420.

Contents

PART II
Key Contacts For Targeting Your Job Search

For my parents Paul and Shirley Merritt without
whose love and guidance I would
not be the man I am today.

Foreward

If you are leaving the government service and looking for a meaningful position in enterprise, this guide developed by Mark Merritt will give you substantive direction in your job search. Mark has covered all the things you will need to face and how to overcome the major challenges you will encounter in finding that "right" job. Of particular importance, his book will bolster your confidence in your ability to make the transition experience a reasonably pleasant one.

Mark's publication provides the pathway and offers ways and means for coping with a very stressful situation. He has thoroughly analyzed the job search process and has packaged a timely and useful handbook that assures success in the pursuit of high quality and self fulfilling employment in what may be an alien culture to you.

As one who has been through the process of leaving government and finding my way into the strange, to me at least, commercial world, I recommend Mark's book without reservation as your guiding light to a successful career.

Carl H. Norton
Deputy Director for Resources and Systems,
Defense Intelligence Agency, GS-17, Retired

Acknowledgments

There are a number of people who helped me write this book. Some know it, some do not. To Paul White, Eric Nelson, Jim Stark, Tim Hosek, Marcus Pierson and Mr. Carl Norton whom provided direct assistance on the book itself. To Jack Moore who helped me in time of need. To Mike Brenton (and Sally) who always kept my best interests in mind. To my brothers Paul Spaulding and Brian Schwarz (and of course their lovely wives and children) for their never ending faith and friendship. To Dave and Diane Dougherty, Jim, Diane and Chrissy Moss, Peter and Stephanie Zwack, Paul and Mette Czarzasty, Jim and Laurie Mousaw (and their wonderful children), Dave and John Conroe, Dave Rittenhouse, Jim Hennessey, John Kaplan, Jeff McCredie, Jeff Irving, Dave Clements, Bobby Fecteau and family, Rick and Karyn Cordier and family all for being great friends. Also Glenn DeSoto and Doug Edgell for being great people to work for. To my sisters Kathy and Karyn just for being you. Special thanks to Zhi Hamby. You know why Zhi. I want to take this opportunity to extend a hearty thanks to all. Writing a book is certainly not an easy task even in the best of times.

Introduction

I believe individuals who have served a tour of duty in the United States military are special, let alone those who made it a career. We are special you know. Blessed by the government of the United States of America to carry out work that is critical to the safety of our great nation, we've been entrusted to keep our nation's secrets and sometimes put our lives on the line. It is a private club and once in, it seems no other work is as satisfying. We are special.

I come from a combination of two of these worlds: Military Special Operations and Intelligence. I was not what is referred to as an "operator" or "shooter" but provided mission critical intelligence information to those who were. This information supported the planning, execution and safe conclusion of missions authorized by the National Command Authority. I chose this course and it provided me a thrill I never experienced before. I found my calling.

Within the Special Operations community any Sea, Air Land (SEAL), US Army Ranger, Air Force or Marine Corps Special Forces "shooter" will tell you, the privilege of being one of the elite does not come easily. It's tough! A great deal of time and tax payers' dollars go into training these national assets. These individuals are screened and tested, driven and finally blessed, to be part of a special club.

Members of the intelligence community are subjected to extremely thorough background investigations. Sometimes, for very sensitive accesses, a background investigation requires us to bare our souls, which can be an uncomfortable experience for the uninitiated.

Many military personnel outside of intelligence or SpecOps obtain security clearances by their proximity to sensitive equipment, information or operations. Many intelligence specialists come from a military background as do most special operations people. Regardless, there comes a time in our lives when we decide to change jobs—be it a military person leaving the service after one or two tours or a professional wanting a change of venue. We all run the same gamut. For those already in the civilian job market it can sometimes be easier. What about those who are entering the civilian job market for the first time? The transition from military to civilian can be mind boggling. Within the military there are strict guidelines that govern how you change jobs, how you look for a new one and qualify for it. Out in the civilian world things follow a different set of rules.

Several things inspired me to write this book. When I decided to leave active duty, I was uncertain of how to market my skills. I knew I wanted to pursue an intelligence-related career. I knew I had experience, clearances and the desire, but the question was, "How do I do it?" I knew about opportunities with Federal agencies, but what else was out there? There was no reference guide unique to the cleared community.

When I became unemployed for a second time. I still had to resort to the basics. But this time I was looking for a job with six years of experience, contacts for networking and knowledge of the system. I started thinking, "What must this be like for someone who doesn't know the system?" It made me think back to when I first got out of the military—no guide then, no guide now.Therefore, based on my job search experience, I wanted to provide something useful for these professionals.

It is for you, the military, intelligence and special operations professionals, who are, or will be, in search of employ within the civilian community that I've written this book. It's designed with your specific employment needs in mind. Every organization noted in this book knows you are out there and they are always looking for highly trained and motivated professionals.

This book is about job search basics and contact information. It attempts to marry military skills and clearances to the civilian job world. It is not another book on resume writing, interviewing or job hunting skills. While the book will not guarantee you a job it will surely get you started on the right foot.

Remember, we are special people who have held special jobs. With this book you should be able to continue pursuing a career you really love.

ALTERNATIVE CAREERS IN SECRET OPERATIONS

1

Lessons Past and Present

Discovering what you love to do and finding jobs that let you do it is easier said than done. If you've ever worked in and out of special operations, you probably know what I mean. We love our work, but our careers are often unpredictable, especially when we leave the military or government to pursue a worklife in the civilian job market.

I come from a very small town in upstate New York. The area is heaven but employment is difficult. I went to undergraduate school to be a high school teacher. After graduating with a B.A. in European History, I went home but was unable to find work. After six months I entered a graduate program in education. During the day I cut fire wood to earn living expenses. In the evening I attended graduate school at St. Lawrence University. The following spring I graduated with a Master's Degree in Human Development.

By the time I graduated, I had decided Secondary Education was not for me. With Master's in hand I applied for entry level administrative positions at local universities. Again, I failed to find full time employment. I was now working construction and getting overcome by school loans, car payments and rent. I was in dire straits when The United States Navy found me.

1

I entered Naval service as an enlisted person with a Masters degree. Now there is a lesson in humility! After six months in a pre-commissioning unit for the aircraft carrier Theodore Roosevelt CVN-71 and a year on a destroyer, I was accepted into intelligence training. Call it what you want—fate, luck or divine intervention—but upon graduation I was screened and accepted into a classified Naval Special Warfare program. I loved the work and soon excelled. Without question, I knew I had finally found my calling.

After four years I began looking beyond the service. I wanted to enter the civilian intelligence community but was unprepared to market my skills. For one thing, I didn't really know what was out there. I contemplated defense contracting, but given the prevailing stigma of "Beltway Bandit" and "sleazy contractor," I avoided this option. After all, I was a highly trained and experienced intelligence analyst.

Fate has a funny way of dashing the plans of mice and men. The year 1990 was the first year of a Federal government hiring freeze. Since I was from outside the "system", the freeze excluded people like me. I heard it over and over again as I knocked on employers' doors: *"You have great experience and credentials, but we cannot hire you."*

Again, call it what you want, with two weeks before leaving the service, no job, one interview and nothing on the horizon, I was hired by a defense contractor. How the gods shined on me that day! But wait, this is a greatly loathed and feared defense contractor—the very epitome of greed and corruption. How can I accept this fate? Well pal, when the mortgage is due you find yourself appeasing the revenuer. I was to be a defense contractor, for now.

I lucked out. The job provided me great experience, travel and contacts. I moved to Europe in support of a US Army counterintelligence mission where I jumped ship to join another contractor. I even went to the former Yugoslavia as one of the first defense contractors to go into that quagmire. Four years later, and well experienced, I returned to the United States. Then it happened again. One year later I was unemployed and writing this book.

We love to say, *"been there, done that."* I went into the community the first time ignorant, the second time experienced, and you know what? The same lessons held true. Believe me, during my second unemployed period (nine weeks) I read the newspapers, cold called people, called in markers, networked my butt off and rewrote my resume and cover letter. Week after week went by. I stopped doing the *"gee, I think I'm a pretty nifty guy"* routine. I got several interviews, but as the weeks went by, my savings disappeared and I was on the last of my credit cards.

Ladies and gentleman of the military services I am here to tell you that unless you have a sugar daddy out there, you will find yourself doing some, if not all, of the recommendations in this book. I lived it twice. During my last lesson in unemployment (and humility), I regained my faith in humanity. Indeed, I was provided assistance by complete strangers, many of whom I cold called. Jack Moore was one who helped. Thanks Jack! There were also those who never lost the faith. Paul White was one. He never stopped trying to get me a job. And he finally succeeded! Thanks Paul.

So let's get on with it my fellow professionals. Go out there and show them you know what you are doing!

Part I

Finding Your New Job

2

The Marketing Plan

Perhaps during a period of deep contemplation, a lucid moment occurred when you decided you knew exactly what you wanted to do when you got off active duty:

> ➤ *I want to continue doing analysis.*

> ➤ *I want to continue supporting the submarine community.*

> ➤ *I want to continue playing with guns.*

> ➤ *I want to keep doing security work.*

> ➤ *I want to keep fighting terrorism.*

You might be six months from getting off active duty or out and already looking. You are trained to think logically and you are organized. While you need to do your homework and take action, things must be done in a certain order. This requires planning and what I call my "marketing plan". It has worked twice for me and I share it with you.

The Plan consists of three fundamental parts: research; the resume and cover letter; and networking to get the word out. **Research** determines who does what and where they are. The **resume and cover letter** introduce you to prospective employers but will not be the same for all jobs and employers. There are elements that you tailor and tune to a specific target audience. **Networking** strengthens your position. It's like insider information. It provides contacts within the community you hope will furnish information, leads, and endorsements. It is source development. You know someone who knows someone who knows someone else. Getting the word out is just that and usually occurs at two levels. It lets prospective employers know you are out there and lets your network know so they can spread the word.

My marketing plan assumes you already know what it is you want to do. Some of you will only have to develop parts of it. Some will be required to start from scratch and work through the whole thing. Regardless, the process is an ongoing one requiring research, writing and distributing resumes and letters, and networking for information, advice, and referrals that result in getting the word out about your employment interests and skills. The key is don't give up. This is but a battle plan. The war remains to be won!

3

Research: Who Does This Stuff?

Before we define "**who**", let's define "**stuff**". Virtually every-thing you learned in your military, intelligence or special operations career is marketable. There are opportunities in intelligence analysis and automation, physical and personal security, surveillance, weapons production, counternarcotics, counterterrorism, demolitions, overhead collection platforms, communications, non-proliferation, weapons of mass destruction (nuclear, chemical biolo-gical warfare), training, law enforcement, security management, intelligence community management, Open Source Intelligence, tech-nical writing, Research and Development, Test and Evaluation, government liaison and all the INT's just to name a few. So **who** does it?

There are two main institutions that hire trained military, intelli-gence or special operations personnel: the government and govern-ment contractors (working for government but not part of govern-ment). I include commercial business with government contracting merely to separate private business from government employment. There is of course a difference between working for a government contractor and working for Levi Strauss, but we will get to that.

Government Positions

At the time of this writing just about all the big government departments and organizations do intelligence work or hire cleared professionals. DoD, CIA, DIA, NSA, DEA, ATF, DOE, DOT, FBI, FEMA, FAA, ARPA, State Department, Secret Service, Customs and Treasury to name a few. Government organizations begin at the federal level and move down through state and local levels. This includes federal law enforcement. There are pro's and con's to working for "Big Brother" but the work is out there. For the most part making application to them is a process which you must engage in directly with them. Application forms for the National Security Agency are not in the *Washington Post*! Each has its own Civilian Personnel Office. Those addresses are included in Chapter 13.

Government Contracting and Commercial Enterprises

Government contractors are private companies paid by the government to provide services that the government is unable to provide itself, for whatever reasons. They read like a cornucopia of names, acronyms, and dark undertones. In this era of government and DoD downsizing, there remains work which the government cannot do itself. We are no longer threatened by the monolith of Soviet communism with the high priority requirement of counting tanks and missiles (though I am sure we do). However, there are just as many "bad guys" doing equally nasty things now as ever before. The leopard did not disappear, he just changed his spots. Now we monitor the transfer of defense technologies, nuclear and fissile material, international terrorism and money transfers, narcotics, illegal immigration, industrial espionage, arms control and international peace keeping missions, not to mention the occasional war. New and old mission requirements continue to present themselves. While the bodies go away, the missions continue. The leopard may have changed its spots but there are still plenty of leopards out there. So how does that affect you, the prospective civilian employee?

It may surprise you to learn that it is cheaper for the government to hire a contractor to do the job of a service member than it is to pay the overall cost for that service member. The government pays for a service member's housing, food, medical, dental, training, transportation and pay, not to mention that of his or her family. With a contractor the government pays an initial flat fee and adds to it as requirements demand. The contractor community flourishes. Before the latest draw down, many contractors were sorely dependent upon government for their survival. By staying flexible and diversifying, most of them were able to continue work both in and out of government.

The commercial environment is similar to government contracting. It provides goods and services just like a contractor but for a different clientele. These companies face many of the same threats as government: espionage, technology transfer, and physical, personal, industrial, communication and automation security. Think about it. How does Levi Strauss, Microsoft or General Dynamics prevent their blue jeans, software or combat aircraft components from being stolen or copied? That's right, someone has to provide security for these industries. Whether it be computer security, physical security, or protection of goods to and from the customer, someone has to do it. Trained professionals are at a premium. We have laws that are supposed to dissuade crime against industry but it is people like you who fill the void by providing professional intelligence and security.

4

Where Are The Jobs and How Do I Find Them?

N ow that I have convinced you there is work in the civilian community, let's turn to identifying where the jobs are and how to find them. We'll start where most job seekers begin—the newspapers.

Newspapers Everywhere

A few government jobs are announced in the newspapers. Application for them is usually carried out through their respective civilian personnel offices. Most job listings are posted within agencies, through Federal Job Information Centers, on agency Web sites, and in special biweekly publications such as the *Federal Career Opportunities* and the *Federal Jobs Digest*. Government contracting jobs, on the other hand, are announced in many places, including newspapers. How many companies advertise is directly proportionate to the amount of government work and facilities in the area. Take Washington, D.C., for example, a Mecca for contractors and the place where the term "Beltway Bandit" was born. Look at any Sunday employment section of the *Washington Post*. The names go on and on. But not all available contracting jobs are advertised. Actually, few are. That is where our network will come to play. Let's look more closely at geographical locations.

Washington DC is a prime example of a geographical location where defense work is in abundance. Why? For one thing Washington is the capital of the free world. Many large corporations have their headquarters here. It is also home to the Armed Services and every branch of the Federal government.

Contracting jobs also are advertised for other geographical areas, inside and outside the continental United States. Part of your decision to leave the service revolved around where you wanted to work. When looking, you should understand that government contracting work does not take place in every small town in America. When searching for it in newspapers, you should look at the big picture first.

Chances are if you pick up the Possum Corners Louisiana Times (yes, there is such a place but I doubt a paper by that name exists) you may not find many government contracting jobs. Start by looking for defense related facilities (airbase, Naval base, training facility, electronic ground station, missile range, etc.) near by. Chances are pretty good you'll see jobs posted. The locations of defense facilities are not the only search criteria. A little research into geographical locations of large corporations will reveal much. Boeing, Lockheed-Martin and General Electric, just to name a few, are so big and handle such huge defense contracts that they don't need to be near a defense facility. They have subsidiary plants all over the country. Many major US cities host defense industries. Do your homework. Find out what companies do defense work, narrow the field and look for names. Chapters 17 and 18 will help you with this task but don't disregard the newspapers.

The US Office of Personnel Management

The U.S. Office of Personnel Management provides detailed information on how to apply for a Federal job. This is how they describe the process: "For job information 24 hours, 7 days a week, call 912/757-3000, the US Office of Personnel Management (OPM) automated telephone system. Or, with a computer modem, dial

912/757-3100 for job information from an OPM electronic bulletin board. You can also reach the board through the Internet (Telnet) at:

FJOB.MAIL.OPM.GOV

"To apply for a Government job review the list of openings, decide which jobs you are interested in, and follow the instructions given. You may apply for most jobs with a resume, **SF-171** or an *Optional Application for Federal Employment*, or any other written format you choose. For jobs that are unique, or filled through automated procedures, you will be given special forms to complete (you can get an *Optional Application* or **SF-171** by calling OPM or dialing the electronic bulletin board at the numbers above)."

The Internet - Intellink

The growth of the InfoHighway, Internet and World Wide Web has created a revolution in open source intelligence and information. I won't bore you with the hype other than say there is a plethora of information out there. The following Web Site is a good example of newspapers currently on-line on the World Wide Web:

http://www.careerpath.com

It provides the Sunday edition Employment sections of, at last count, nineteen national newspapers: *Boston Globe, Chicago Tribune, Los Angeles Times, New York Times, San Jose Mercury News, Washington Post,* etc. Chapter 14 provides other valuable sites to direct your searches and new sources are added to the Web daily!

For those of you still presently cleared, the Intellink is a must! Just about everyone involved in the community has a Web Page. All DoD MACOM's, government and Federal agencies and most organizations involved in defense and intelligence have Web Sites. Many list ongoing projects, efforts and some (DIA) list job opportunities. Due to the nature of Intellink, I cannot go into further detail; but if you have access, it is an amazing resource.

The Community

One major benefit I hope you will get from this book is the realization that there is an extensive network of organizations and people, which make up the existing intelligence community, you can tap into. What do I mean by community? This refers to a rather defined collection of government agencies, private companies, publications and people who work in the craft of intelligence. At first glance the intelligence community seems like a vast web, but once you start working your way around it you will be pleasantly surprised at how small it really is. You will be making calls and getting to know people. All of the sudden half the people you have just met know the other half you already know! The fifth contact down the line will know the first one you met. The deeper you go the more you realize how tightly knit the whole thing is. This works as a benefit to you but you need to start somewhere.

People who have been in the community a long time are usually the best to search out. For instance, the last time I was unemployed (this is also called being "between jobs" for those of you who find the term "unemployed" unsavory), I went to my professional intelligence association journals and sought out names. I then went to the membership directory and cross referenced. I called the ones I knew and cold called the ones I didn't. This led to a further list of contacts. Before I knew it I was invited to the Carl Norton Intelligence Roundtable luncheon with over fifty intelligence professionals! Bingo!

Chapter 10 includes addresses of professional organizations within the community. I recommend joining as many as you qualify for. You cannot join them all. Some have criteria. The Marine Corps Counterintelligence Association, for example, is one who will only let individuals join who have been to an official military CI school. They are made up of community professionals, just like you, representing years of knowledge and experience, many of whom have been exactly where you are today. These are contacts to cultivate. They are friendly and helpful and represent the very essence of what you need, people in the know. You will be amazed at how many contacts can be made through these organizations. They are the foundation of your research.

Chapter 10 also provides a list professional journals and publications. A wealth of knowledge can be obtained by subscribing to them . For example, the American Defense Preparedness Associations journal *National Defense* provides a tremendous amount of information on the military and intelligence community (names, addresses, contractors, etc.). Most are dedicated to the defense establishment and the military—what it is doing, new projects and developments, who is doing the work and where they are. They also provide the vision for the community in the coming century. Read and pay heed! This is a guiding light. It includes what kinds of expertise will be needed and where the resources will be applied. Once you get that job, these publications will help you continue to do your work. They spell out plain and simple what the military is thinking about and who is thinking about it. Just follow the light.

DoD Announcements

I know at the time of this writing you can walk into the main lobby of The Defense Intelligence Agency (DIA) on Bolling Air Force Base, Washington, DC and find a book containing current DIA employment opportunities. You don't need a clearance to get that far, but you will need a clearance to get to their Civilian Personnel Office (CPO). All government organizations have CPO's. Some have regularly updated voice recordings of current jobs available. Call them and ask for help. They will be glad to and are a wealth of information. Remember, they are in the work force already. The phone numbers for many CPO's and voice recordings are found in Chapter 11.

Professional Publications

Several commercial publications list available government positions. One of the best is *Federal Career Opportunities* which lists thousands of currently available federal jobs, nationwide and overseas, GS grades through SES. Updated and published every two weeks, it includes jobs organized by occupational groups and series with mailing addresses, contact names and phone numbers. The *Federal Career Opportunities* is published by Federal Research Service (243 Church Street, Suite 200, Vienna, VA 22180-4434, Tel. 703/281-

0200). The company also offers an electronic version of *Federal Career Opportunities*, KSA workbooks and application preparation software with SF-171 and OF-612 forms.

5

The Resume and Cover Letter

How do you plan to communicate your qualifications to employers who know little or nothing about you? You'll need to write resumes and letters that target your skills on employers' needs.

How Do I Apply What I Know?

The key to applying what you know is to take a realistic view of what you want to do. If you are looking for a job where you throw hand grenades all day, your definition may be a little too defined (though it would not surprise me if there was a job out there like that). If, however, you could envision that you would like to work in the explosive ordnance industry, then you might be a little better off. The same goes for most other skills you learned from your respective communities. If you can generalize somewhat, you can tailor your requirements and research options.

Define generally and refine. I call this "Tailoring and Targeting". If you are a pilot and want to fly for the community, that is pretty simple. If you are an intelligence analyst for the Middle East and you want to continue doing that, pretty easy as well. However, the person

18

with many skills needs to define and refine. Choose a general area of expertise. Glean out relevant experience, refine it and apply it to a target set. Your research phase will be guided by how you do this. Look in those areas for companies and organizations who do this kind of work. When you have found out who does it, target that audience. This will also guide how you write your resume.

If you look at examples of commercial job opportunities and government positions, you will learn a great deal about job options relevant to your interests, skills, and experience. Most jobs revolve around areas of expertise. Look for buzz words. Here are some actual newspaper advertisements for opportunities in the community:

Network Engineer, Database Specialist, Trainer, Hardware/ Software Engineers, Research Analysts, Threat Intelligence Analysts, Systems Analysis and Design, Wireless Services Engineer, Information Systems Architectures, Military Analyst, Project Manager, Business Process Reengineering Consultants, UNIX System Administrators, Operations Research Analyst, Air/Ground Forces Analysts, Senior Organizational Effective- ness Consultant, GOTS Analysts, C4I Engineers, WAN/LAN Engineers, Information Engineers, Legacy System Migration, Transportation Engineers.

The titles go on and on. Read these carefully and glean out the essentials. What are they asking for and how? Doing this type of analysis will help tremendously when it comes time to write your resume. Remember, tailor and target.

If you served in the United States military you certainly did not have to write a resume to get that job! Oh you did paper work all right, but if you didn't have a resume prior to entering the service you may never have had the opportunity (or nightmare) of writing one. Regardless, you now have special skills you need to present in resume format. Before we start, let's take a moment to discuss some theory regarding resumes.

You'll find numerous books on the market devoted to resume writing. My intent here is to provide a few basic principles to get you started. There are certain things you should know about the process. You have enormous freedom and flexibility in how you present your background, as long as your resume is well organized, inviting to read and convincingly conveys your qualifications.

You should write a resume that stands out from the crowd, one that will be placed in the "call this candidate" pile and not the circular file. Many questions need to be answered: How many pages should my resume be? Is it too long or short? What kind of paper should I use? Do I double space? Should I use fancy lettering? What do I put in a cover letter? Let's start by dispelling some myths about resumes.

MYTH 1:　　**A resume should be only one page long**.

REALITY:　Your resume is a marketing tool designed to produce job interviews. If you are in your 20's and have only held one or two jobs, a one-page resume will be sufficient. However if you have decades of experience, you'll need two pages at least to do justice to your background (and even then you really need about four!). There seems to be a common understanding that you not go over two pages with a resume. Sometimes the pure volume of resumes that a prospective employer receives precludes him from reading every word of every resume that crosses his desk. Most resume readers usually scan for highlights (15 seconds) only to determine whether the candidate is called or not. To facilitate the quick scan you want to make your resume as easy on the reader as possible.

MYTH 2:　　**A resume shouldn't include a job objective.**

REALITY:　Many people fiercely debate whether resumes should contain objective statements. Some believe objective statements limit the types of positions for which candidates can be considered. However, on the other hand, by leaving out this statement, you may appear to be without direction, desperate to grab any position that comes along. I say, let them know up front. Honesty is the best policy and the most expeditious. Begin with an objective or summary paragraph. Keep it brief and to the point. Follow this with your education. Next your chronological work history. Start with your most recent job and list backward. Again be brief and to the point. Experience should always be presented in short sentences preceded by bullets. If you have a great deal of technical experience and training you may want to highlight this in a separate list. This should be placed after the objective paragraph. It is these skills you want to highlight up front. Don't make the reader search for important details in mounds of descriptive text. Follow your work history with clearances held (date of SSBI, polygraph etc.).

MYTH 3: **A resume shouldn't contain any personal information.**

REALITY: If it is not pertinent to the job for which you are applying, leave it off. However, added personal information about your abilities can substantially enhance your perceived qualifications if you hope to make a career change. Include details about personality traits you possess that show how you would succeed in your desired job. An example for an Open Source Intelligence Analyst: author of the book entitled "Employment Guide for Military, Intelligence and Special Operations Community Personnel in The Civilian Job Market." Not directly related to the job, but guess what? The information in the book was all derived from Open Sources! See what I mean?

How you present your data on paper will impact the ease by which it is read. Bolding and capital letters and italics should be used to highlight important points. When describing work performed, follow the **KISS** principal: <u>K</u>eep <u>I</u>t <u>S</u>imple <u>S</u>tupid! Keep away from long descriptions. Stay away from "Buzz Words" and undefined acronyms. Remember, you want to grab the readers attention and keep it, not put them to sleep.

Make sure you do not get locked into myths about the "correct" or "only way" to describe your experience on your resume. You always have flexibility as long as your resume convincingly conveys your capabilities and will prompt employers to schedule an interview. Begin by stating the job description held (ex. Chief, Counterintelligence Division, NCOIC Patriot Missile Battery, Head Analyst, South/Central America). Under the description note your distinguishing accomplishments; time/money saved, manpower retention, problems tackled and solved. Remember, note your work experience chronologically and only the last ten years. An important rule to follow is one which we all learned in military training: **Attention To Detail**! Nothing can defeat you quicker than misspellings, typographical or grammatical errors. This reflects upon you!

Your "Tickets" Are The Ticket

Employment opportunities are dependent upon environmental influences—what the market is like and whether or not we are at war, political climate and budget constraints, the end of the fiscal year or the ever present government job freeze. They all have an effect on your own ability to get a job in the community.

One thing in your favor is your security clearance. Those of you who have been cleared know that it is not easy, and it is always time consuming, to get one. Depending, once again, on environmental constraints, you may find you are in effect selling your clearance and not necessarily your expertise. That is okay. When it comes down to working or not working, your first priority is paying the bills! You might not get the perfect job the first time out, but you can use your clearance to your benefit and market yourself in the door.

If you recall Chapter 3, "Lessons Past and Present," when I got my first contracting job, it was because I had a general knowledge of a computer system **and** because I was cleared! I had no aspirations of doing computer work. That was not one of my strengths. As a matter of fact, I actually disliked computers but enjoyed the people in the community who used them. I was cleared and in the door. Times would change and once in I could more favorably position myself. Before I knew it I had spent four glorious years in Europe and added a whole new area of expertise, counterintelligence, to my resume! The moral is, *"if you have them keep them."* They are a door opener. Do not worry that the only thing available is not your life's work. Get your foot in the door. The rest will follow.

No One Sells You Better Than You

You are your own best salesman! Only you know what you know and what you have done. Obviously you want to paint yourself in as pretty a picture as possible but sometimes you can paint yourself into a corner.

Follow all the rules described above. What you write will come out in the interview. DO NOT lie or exaggerate. Your references and previous employers will be called! Be professional in describing all important skills, training and experience. There will be nothing that kills you quicker than to put something in a resume which is a half or partial truth. If you are a subject matter expert by all means say so. If, on the other hand, you say you have a familiarity with a certain area be sure you can qualify it. Chances are you will be asked. Being familiar with a subject does not mean you are an expert. It merely suggests that somewhere in your training or experience you have dealt with this area. Careful use of words can make all the difference in the world.

If you are a young and less experienced candidate, one thing that will help you is to look for things in your past you may have overlooked. For instance, do not downplay the fact that you were an enlisted person. Enlisted personnel in the United States military carry great responsibility. As you advanced in rank so did your responsibilities. You supervised people and were responsible for expensive equipment. These are management skills and responsibilities not to be overlooked. I have one friend who, after getting out of the Marine Corps as an E5, got a job as a manager of a CompUSA outlet at $45,000 a year. This was based on his enlisted management experience from the Corps! This was not the intelligence community but it proves a point.

I know a sailor who was an E5 Petty Officer in charge of the forward gun mount on a Spruance Class Destroyer while on active duty. He was not going to make mention of this fact in his resume. He was responsible for making sure the right kinds of munitions got into the breech of that forward mount, an extremely key weapon system on a Spruance Class. Not only was he responsible for providing the right munitions but was responsible for making sure three other men did the same. He was responsible for the smooth running of a vital weapon system and the safety and well being of three men in preparation for war time operations. He was chosen because he was bright and responsible. If he failed, he could have put the entire ship and crew in jeopardy. He demonstrated leadership and responsibility.

Another thing to look at is your past training experience. Military personnel today receive the most advanced system and weapons training of any nation in the world. You are preparing yourself to go out into the industry that makes that equipment. Do not neglect to specify what equipment or platform you worked on or that you were training NCO or POIC for your Platoon, Company or Division. These are important skills to bring to the table. Automation and communications are highly sought after areas of expertise today. If you fixed it, built it, or trained it, chances are someone needs you to do it for them. Programmers are worth a bundle. Bring these skills out. Remember, no one sells you better than you!

Tailor and Target - Do Your Homework

Here we are back to Tailor and Target. It is as important when doing your searches as it is in writing your resume and cover letter. You want to highlight why you stand out as a candidate. You have found the target. Now direct your message at the target. Let's start with the cover letter.

The cover letter is an introduction to an employer. It states your intention and targets the specific position for which you are applying. Read carefully all advertisements or job announcements. What are they asking for? Tailor your letter to respond exactly to their requirement. If you have the skills they desire, and can qualify them in the resume, state it. Give them what they want. Intrigue them into wanting to spend more than fifteen seconds on your resume. It will mean the difference between the "to call" pile or the circular file. The letter should be no more than a paragraph or two. Be clear and concise. Remember, the goal here is to get the reader to read the resume.

Float Like A Butterfly, Sting Like a Bee

I know this may sound corny, but it is exactly what you are going to do. Sending resumes to potential employers is sometimes called "floating paper." All this means is "getting the paper out." How you do this is up to you but there are productive and unproductive ways of doing it. It reemphasizes the need to research, tailor, target and write good "paper." Let's take a moment to examine what happens to that resume after it hits the receiving end.

Usually your resume will be received by a Human Resource (HR) person. In some big firms an HR office will get between two hundred fifty and three hundred resumes a day. They are supposed to see that it gets to the project managers (PM's) whose requirements you are responding to. Once the program managers get it, hopefully they read it. Most times the read may be no more than a fifteen second scan. At that time they will put your resume in a "call or can" pile. Most companies will send you a little card or letter explaining that your resume was received, that your skills are being weighed against current requirements and that you will be contacted if a match is made. Some companies don't even send you a reply. You will not know if it got to the intended audience or not. But you receive a card and are now content your resume is in the hands of competent individuals. You are sure you will be receiving a phone call. Regardless whether you receive a response or not, many things can happen to your resume along the way.

Let us say HR has a bad day. We all have them. They receive it and send you a card or letter telling you as much. But say they mishandle it, file it incorrectly, lose it, or just plain destroy it by accident. As far as you know it got to the people you intended. After all, you have a receipt telling you it did. Let us say HR gets it to the appropriate program managers and the PM has a bad day. We all have them. Let's say they misplace it, or due to the sheer volume of responses they don't have time to review it. You really won't know one way or the other what happens to it. You won't know that it might have disappeared into the ozone. You know they got it and feel content that being such a strong candidate you will surely be called. After all, who could read your resume and not call you! This can lead to something we will discuss shortly called the *"Gee, didn't anyone read my resume"* syndrome.

How you put your resume out on the street is important. There is a right way and a wrong way. Either you have done your homework and targeted a select audience or you do what is referred to as "Blanketing" which probably means one of two things; You just don't care **who** gets it or, you don't know who **should** get it. Blanketing signifies laziness and lack of doing one's homework. There are consequences to this.

If you send your resume to just anyone, it will be apparent to those who read it that you are "fishing" for work. You don't care what either of you has to offer; you just want a job. You can burn bridges with this approach. If HR receives your misguided resume they will know what you are doing. If they continue to receive it, week after week, surely that bridge is blown. If the time ever comes when you actually target this company with something to offer, they probably won't even give it the time of day. You will have been marked. These are reasons why it is important to do your homework. Research, tailor and target, and get the paper out. Float your paper gently and correctly. Your efforts will be rewarded.

Applying For a Federal Job

The following Federal application guidelines come from the U.S. Office of Personnel Management's publication, *Working For America Works For You: A Guide to Federal Careers in Washington, DC.*

There are a few basic things you should know about Federal jobs before you start applying for one. The Federal Government has several different pay systems. The General Schedule (GS) is the largest pay system. It covers most white collar jobs and consists of 15 numerical grade levels and their corresponding salaries. Under this system, certain jobs have special salary rates. Some jobs in the Federal service do not fall under the GS pay system. The Federal Wage Grade (WG) pay system covers blue collar jobs in apprentice and journeyman trades and crafts occupations. The Senior Executive

Schedule (ES) covers high level managerial and supervisory positions in the Federal Government's Senior Executive Service (SES).

Eligibility for Federal jobs is determined by your education and work experience. With a high school degree you will usually qualify for GS-2 grade level positions. To qualify for the GS-5 or GS-7 grade levels in professional and administrative positions you need a Bachelor's degree or three years of increasingly responsible work experience after high school. If you have an undergraduate grade point average of 3.0 or higher, or membership in an academic honor society, you may qualify for the GS-7 level based on "Superior Academic Achievement". Applicants with Masters degrees are eligible for the GS-9 grade level and those with Doctoral degrees may be considered at the GS-11 level. Grade levels for professional and administrative positions under the GS pay system increase first in 2-grade intervals (ex. GS-5,7,9,11) and then in 1-grade intervals (ex. GS-12,13,14,15). Each grade increase typically means a salary increase of several thousand dollars.

Federal **competitive** service means applicants compete for positions based on a written exam and/or evaluation of their education and work experience. However, some occupations, such as lawyer, chaplain and certain agencies such as CIA and the General Accounting Office are **excepted** from these procedures. Excepted agencies determine their own criteria for accepting and evaluating applications. If you want to apply for excepted positions or to excepted agencies contact the individual agencies personnel office.

The US Office of Personnel Management (OPM) develops and implements policies about personnel issues and activities for the Federal Government's competitive service. In addition to its headquarters the OPM has five regional offices and a number of service centers around the country. You can find these listed in Chapter 13 of this book. These offices are responsible for conducting OPM functions such as recruitment and job information in their locations.

The Washington Area Service Center (WASC) provides service for the Washington, DC metropolitan area. If you are looking for a Federal job in this area, your first step should be to contact WASC's Federal Job Information Center (FJIC) in OPM's headquarters building located at 1900 E Street, NW in room 1416. There are many FJIC's across the country that provide information about Federal employment in specific geographical locations. Since application procedures for Federal jobs may vary throughout the country you should contact the FJIC nearest where you would like to work to find out about specific paths to employment in that area. A list of nation-wide FJIC's is located in the Annex of this book.

At a FJIC you can get information about jobs as well as forms and application material you may need. Job vacancies are advertised at the FJIC in a weekly publication called the Federal Job Opportunities Listing (FJOL). The FJOL advertises positions that are open and tells you who to call for additional information. The FJOL is also posted in State Employment Service offices.

You can use the automated telephone and touch screen computers or talk directly with an information specialist to learn about Federal employment opportunities and application procedures. The FJIC is open Monday through Friday, 8 a.m. to 4 p.m. daily. The automated telephone line 202/606-2700 provides job information 24 hours a day, 7 days a week. It offers a menu of recorded information including job vacancy listings (code 406). You can request applications and other forms on this line (code 280) and talk to an information specialist during business hours (code 000) about your specific questions.

Agencies in the Washington, DC metropolitan area fill their vacancies in a variety of ways, sometimes independently of OPM. For many Federal jobs you must apply directly for vacancies advertised by agencies, and for others, you must take an entry level test. The first step is to find out which of the following procedures is the right one for your field and contact the FJIC.

Your military service may count as general or specialized experi-ence when applying for civilian positions. Additionally as a veteran you may receive preference in obtaining Federal employment. If you are qualified for the position you want, Veterans Preference will add either 5 or 10 points to the numerical evaluation of your applications. The FJIC also has a veterans employment counselor who can be reached on 202/606-1848.

The **Standard Form 171, Application for Federal Employment** is the government form to make application for their positions. The government has even added a new form for those who do not wish to complete a 171. It is the **Optional Application for Federal Employment—OF 612**. A shorter version of the 171, it elicits the general information. Samples of both documents are in the back of this book. The Federal government will also accept your resume but it must include all pertinent information contained in the 171. We will address this issue shortly but first the 171.

There is nothing particularly daunting about the 171 other than it is painstaking to fill out. The best software program designed specifically for creating the SF 171 is the ***Quick and Easy Federal Application Kit*** (Data Tech) that also includes the OF 612 and federal resume formats. Most form maker software today contains standard government forms. "Forms Engine" and "Delrina Form Flow" are two that come to mind. Suffice it to say it is another Standard Form, pure and simple. The trick is, if you haven't been in the system and gotten some 171 experience behind you, your first attempts can be a little rough. A poor 171 writer is often times less competitive than a more learned one. Take my advice. Find someone in government who has experience at it. Human Resource and Civilian Personnel Office personnel usually know the deal pretty well. Middle and upper level management are the real experts as they had to do their own and read those of prospective employees. If all else fails there are any number of books on the market devoted to the 171 application.

A 171 is much like a resume. It provides background information in a particular format. The first time out you will encounter the same problem with the 171 as with a resume. What do I put in, leave out, and how do I word it? The same rules hold for both. Keep it concise and to the point. Use bullets when possible. Include important professional and technical schooling and do not be afraid to ask for help.

The U.S. Office of Personnel Management continues in offering advice on applying for a Federal Job:

> Although the Federal government does not require a standard application form for most jobs, they do need certain information to evaluate your qualifications and determine if you meet legal requirements for Federal employment. If your resume or application does not provide all the information requested in the job vacancy announcement you may lose consideration for a job. Help speed the selection process by keeping your resume or application brief and by sending only the requested material.

Type or print clearly in ink. Include the job information, Announcement number, title and grade(s) for the job you are applying for. Next your personal information. Full name, mailing address (with zip) and day and night time phone numbers (with area code). Social Security Number, country of citizenship, veterans preference, reinstatement eligibility and highest Federal civilian grade held. Next is your education. Begin with your High School name, city and state (Zip code) and the date of your diploma or GED. Colleges and Universities with name, city, state, majors and type and year of any degrees received. Do not send transcripts unless the job vacancy announcement requests it. Your work experience is next. Include experiences for any paid or non-paid work experience related to the job for which you are applying. Include job title, duties and accomplishments, employer's name and address, supervisor's name and phone number, starting and ending dates (month and year), hours per week and salary. Indicate if the government may contact your supervisors. Finally, you will need to provide any other qualifications which are relevant to the position. Job related training courses, skills, languages, computer hardware or software, tools, machinery, typing speed and related certificates and licenses. Do not forget to include job related honors, awards and special accomplishments. Publications, memberships in professional or honor societies, leadership activities, public speaking and performance awards. The following are examples of requirements for the Department of Treasury, United States Secret Service and Alcohol, Tobacco and Firearms (ATF) Agent positions.

The Secret Service hires employees as Special Agents and Uniformed Division Officers and in various Professional, Administrative, Technical and Clerical occupations. Most positions, other than those of Special Agent, are located in the Washington, DC area. To be considered for most positions, you must (a) have reinstatement eligibility based on previous civilian Federal service, or (b) be currently employed in the Federal Government under a career or career-conditional appointment, or (c) have established eligibility in an appropriate office of Personnel Management Register.

Once you have established basic eligibility, you may apply

for specific positions by submitting a Standard Form 171, Application for Federal Employment; or an Optional Form 612, Optional Application for Federal employment; or a resume which must include the information cited in the Office of Personnel Management (OPM) requirement, Optional Form 510, applying for a Federal job. If you submit an Optional Form 612 or a resume, you must also submit an Optional Form 306, Declaration for Federal Employment. These forms are available in all Federal Job Information Centers and in Government Personnel Offices.

Starting salaries for selected grade levels are as follows:

GS-2	$14,498	GS-6	$22,147
GS-3	$15,820	GS-7	$24,610
GS-4	$17,759	GS-9	$30,106
GS-5	$19,869	GS-11	$36,426

Uniformed Division Officer $29,962 (5)

The Department of the Treasury, United States Secret Service, provides this advice on applying for a Federal job:

The Bureau of Alcohol, Tobacco and Firearms (ATF) Treasury Enforcement Agent must first pass the Treasury Enforcement Agent (TEA) examination which is given by your local Office of Personnel Management. Once the examination is passed, your name is placed on a roster of eligible candidates by score order. When the Bureau requests certification of candidates from the OPM, OPM sends a list of the top 4 or 5 candidates to the Bureau. The Bureau then makes a tentative selection from the list. A permanent offer of employment is contingent upon the successful completion of a full field background investigation, a comprehensive medical examination and a drug test.

The experience and educational requirements for an Agent at the GS-5 or GS-7 level are as follows: (a) have a college degree from an accredited college or university; or (b) for the GS-5 level, 3 years of general investigative or law enforcement work which required knowledge and application of laws relating to criminal violations; have the ability to deal effectively with individuals or groups; ability to collect and assemble pertinent facts and to prepare clear and concise written reports. For the GS-7 grade level; One year of specialized experience equivalent to the GS-5 grade level which is defined as experience related to investigation of criminal violations that proved the following:

- Leadership of, or membership in, a military intelligence or criminal investigative team or component in which the principal duties consisted of security investigation, intelligence gathering or criminal prosecution.
- Analyzing or evaluating raw investigative data and preparing comprehensive written investigative reports.
- Investigating criminal cases requiring the use of recognized investigative methods and techniques, and that may have included appearing in court to present evidence.
- Supervising or conducting interviews or interrogations that involved eliciting evidence, data, or surveillance information.
- Law enforcement work in which 50 percent or more of the time involved criminal investigations requiring the use of surveillance, undercover, or other criminal detection methods or techniques.

KSA's

KSA stands for **K**nowledge, **S**kills and **A**bilities. When completing your 171 be sure to address the specific KSA's outlined in the vacancy announcement. Because KSA's are necessary for successful performance on the job, they are used to evaluate qualified applicants. Remember to include volunteer work as work experience.

6

Network, Network, Network
Get the Word Out

Now that you have defined your goals, done your research and represented yourself well on paper, you have to get the word out. How will you do this? Are you going to rely on sending resumes and letters in the mail or will you make contacts through other means?

Friends in Distant Places

We spoke of the "network" earlier. This is where it becomes important. It is all about whom you know—friends, contacts, organization members and professional associates. They all constitute your net-work and you will need to use it to your utmost.

Friends in the community are the best to start with. You know and trust them. You value their judgment and trust them to give you sound advice. Announce to them your intentions. Describe what you want to do and where. Begin by asking if they know anyone directly involved in the kind of work you are interested in. This is networking.

Ask your friends. This is what friends are for.

You should join one or more professional organizations. Use this to establish your next level of contacts. Some fellow members you know already. Call them. Next, read the organizations' newsletters and journals. Choose some names and call them. These are "cold calls" and can be a little uncomfortable sometimes but for the most part you will find your community members willing to help or at least lead you to someone they know who can. All professional organizations produce a newsletter or journal of some sort. I have seen some carry personal availability announcements. Policies on this vary from organization to organization but I have seen at least three in the past.

You have spent time working in your field and made professional contacts outside of friends and association members. Contractors who have worked your site or on your equipment. Call these people. You may not know this but most companies give recruitment bonuses to their employees for bringing in new hires. This can be lucrative. I have seen fees range from $800.00 to $2,500.00! This is like a headhunter's finder fee. If a headhunter is the one responsible for placing you in a company, the company in turn will pay him the finder's fee. The professional search firm will usually receive between 15% and 20% of the find's first year salary. That is how they make their money. For the most part a company would rather see their employees reap the benefit. You are a money maker for them. Unless they are well off, they will probably do everything they can to see if they can't find something and make a little Christmas money in the process.

The Internet and E-Mail

If you are on-line, it can be a tremendously useful job search forum. In the open source Internet environment, as we have discussed earlier, there are a myriad of DoD and government organizations who have Home Pages. Search them out. Use your Search Engine to run key word queries. Telenetting into community Bulletin Boards is very useful to post your availability and there are many job postings on the World Wide Web. Almost all commercial enterprises have Web pages and they have requirements, just like government. Most everyone these days seems to have e-mail, whether on Internet or military networks. Search them out and fire off a short memo stating your requirements. It is free after all.

The Reserves

The Military Reserves is one of the best places to network and develop sources. One thing the reserves represent, outside of a ready military force, is a large representation of the community. We are working professionals representing a huge cross section of government and business—a gold mine of contacts. I have been in the Naval Reserves for over six years since getting off active duty. During that time I have served with one or more representatives of every government intelligence organization and community contractor in the Washington DC area. On top of that I am a member of Naval Intelligence Professionals who promote networking within its rank and file. If you are not a member DO NOT, I repeat DO NOT, use their membership directory for personal gain. You must be a member and will be asked upon application if you wish to participate in their networking function. This goes for any of the community organizations or associations you find in this book. They know who you are and want you to utilize them, but do not abuse the privilege!

7

Alternate Resources

You can conduct a job search on your own by networking and responding to vacancy announcements. However, you also may want to work with professionals who recruit for employers (headhunters or executive search firms) or assist you in developing and implementing your job search (job search and career management firms).

Community Headhunters

Call them what you want, headhunters or executive search specialists are recruiters. They have positions to fill and you may be what their client needs.

A few headhunters cater to the intelligence community exclusively. As members of a private club, they all know one another and have extensive contacts throughout the community. Since they get paid by employers (25-35% of your first-year salary), headhunters primarily work for employers. Nonetheless, most have your interests in mind. After all, they need to work with individuals who have the right combination of skills to fill positions for which they recruit. Without contacts with the right qualified candidates, they can't do business with employers.

Contacting a headhunter by no means guarantees you a job. They network just like you. They will be the first to tell you that. They have requirements provided by any number of businesses or companies which they try hard to fill. The more they fill, the more money they make. Their requirements are prioritized by immediacy, technical levels and other variables. They will enter you somewhere on that scale. Personal contacts will always be your strongest asset so continue to work developing your own network. This provides the best results.

Job Search and Career Marketing Firms

During your job search, you will come across what is variously referred to as job search and career marketing firms. It's important to know what these groups are and what you can expect them to do for you. These firms usually advertise at the beginning of most newspaper employment sections as follows: *"Professionals & Executives Seeking $30,000 to $300,000", "Managers/Executives/Professionals Seeking $50,000 to $350,000", "Finding $85,000 + Positions"*. They are not headhunters because they do not recruit for employers. What you may not know at first glance is that these companies charge you a fee and they can be very expensive. Let me be clear that I am neither knocking nor promoting these companies. I merely want to make you aware of these services and what you can expect to pay and get for your money.

Job search and career marketing firms operate much like an actor's manager. Serving as a career coach who provides advice and structure for conducting an effective job search, they work with and for you. For a fee they take you, train you and manage you. Their services range from conducting assessment testing and helping write your resume to showing you how to dress and conduct yourself in an interview (video taped dress rehearsals), where to search for opportunities, and how to negotiate the offer. For individuals entering the job market for the first time, these can be useful services, but they come at a price—$3,500.00 to $4,500.00 depending upon the contract you sign. For this you will be guided and assisted through many of the processes described in this and other job search books, sometimes over several years depending upon your contract. First-time consultation is usually free. Remember, these are not headhunters since they do not work for employers nor provide you with job opportunities. They are professional career coaches who charge you for their services whether or not you land a job.

8

The "Gee, Didn't Anyone Read My Resume" Syndrome

I love this part. I lived it twice! This will guarantee to put that *"I thought I was a pretty nifty guy or gal"* outlook into perspective. You are faxing and mailing lots resumes. You've prepared well, formulated a good resume and cover letter, did your research, and got your fax numbers and addresses. The jobs are out there and you are applying for them. You are wired. You got a few interviews but applied for over thirty positions. Time rolls on. What's wrong? *"I'm a nifty guy or gal." "Didn't anyone read my resume?"*

Overcome By Events

Alas, the hand of fate is sometimes not a kind one. Yes, you probably are a neat guy or gal and yes, you probably did everything just right, and yes those HR people are not calling you! Let me share a few stories which may explain your frustration. It's called **overcome by events** and there is just nothing you can do about it.

The first time I went out into the civilian intelligence community was 1990. Wouldn't you know but it was the first year of a Federal hiring freeze. It was hard enough for those in the system to move around let alone anyone from the outside. I had a Federal Career Opportunities Guide and saw all Government vacancies world wide. I was pumping out 171's and didn't even know the freeze was in effect. That's when I ended up working for my first government contractor. How was I to know that the Government would put a freeze on hiring. I was **overcome by events**!

The second time I was overcome was while writing this book. I was "between jobs." I was experienced, floating paper and networked tight, I mean wired. It seemed the more paper I put out, the fewer responses I got. Finally two things dawned on me. There was something about the time frame which stood out. I was looking for work during the summers biggest vacation period. No one around. It was August, dawning on September. For the uninitiated this is also the end of the fiscal year. Budgeted government money has been spent and until 1 October, the beginning of the new fiscal year, contracting officers are without it. Contractors won't work at risk so things get real slow. Slow is not the word when it's happening to you. It's death! I was **overcome by events**!

Stay Motivated

I know I cannot lecture members of the military community about motivation, nor anyone else for that matter. You would not be who you are today if not for motivation. Motivation during training is one thing. You know there is a light at the end of a certain time frame and all you have to do is see it through. When looking for a job, you just don't know what that time frame will be. When you are doing everything right and nothing happens life can be extremely frustrating. Take it from me. Staying motivated is the key to getting that job. Persistence is paramount and patience is critical. As wired as you might think you are, there are environmental considerations which you must deal with. We have discussed it. Keep making phone calls and contacts. The more people you talk to, the more people you will meet, and the more you will learn. I have had extremely low points but, through it all, I had people out there working for me. Do not lose sight. It is easier for couples with two incomes. For a single person you can find yourself tapped out and on the desperate side. Do not despair. Keep the faith. Above all, keep working at it. Hard work always pays off!

Follow Through

While you are out there beating the bushes, it is very important to follow through. Once you have made initial contact, pursue it. Do not become a nuisance but always follow up a meeting, or resume application, with a phone call. People you meet have their own lives. Sure you are important to them, but they can get overwhelmed too. Give them a little reminder. Check up on them. They may have a new contact for you but have just not gotten back to you. Remember, they have a job though you do not. They have responsibilities and meetings and phone calls and families. Follow through.

Tips For the Over 50

When you are over the age of 50, job hunting can either be a piece of cake (as we say in the military) or it can be a challenge. Some of you may have discovered how hard it is to get interviews with managers who view more experienced applicants as expensive, set-in-their-ways and technically lacking. Do not add insult to injury! Thinking along these lines can become a self-fulfilling end to the means. Focus on your assets and be positive when seeking new opportunities. Here are a few tips I hope will help

1. **Know what you want and develop a strategy to achieve it.** Start your search by creating an effective and thorough plan of action. Research positions and industries that are of interest to you. Identify employers, define what you can offer, decide what you need to earn, create a marketing plan (chap. 2) and evaluate your interviewing skills.

2. **Control fear before it controls you.** Learning and experiencing new things is often scary. Ward off these fears by staying focused on your goals.

3. **Update your language.** Don't start networking or meeting with employers until you have learned the current buzz-words and trends in your target industry.

4. **Dress for today.** Men, are you wearing polyester slacks or jackets or shiny 3-piece suits? Women, are you stuck in a time warp with teased, sprayed hair, too much makeup and spike heals? Evaluate your appearance. Does it fit the industry, environment or culture you are targeting?

5. **Create a "youthful" resume.** Your resume should cover only your last ten years of experience, not your entire career. The theory is that what you have done recently best illustrates your experience and achievements and builds on everything you did earlier.

6. **Become a savvy interviewer.** Practice thinking on your feet so you'll respond to difficult questions and bounce back from blunders. Remember, everyone makes mistakes, regardless of age. Learn to think creatively when you goof and then move on.

7. **Be prepared to deal with misconceptions about older employees.** Recognize that you will be expected to have: bad attitude, poor health, fear of technology, poor skill match and lack of commitment. These perceptions are inaccurate. To defeat them demonstrate with words and body language during networking meetings and interviews that you are enthusiastic, flexible and have lots of energy.

8. **Tap available resources**. When seeking a new position, (you have already started by using this book!) start by tapping into electronic career databases via a computer. Use your professional organizations, make phone calls and read the newspapers.

Ten Questions *YOU* Ask During Job Interviews

Most candidates know that preparing for interviews is essential. Too often candidates believe preparation includes only showing up on time, dressing professionally and answering the employer's questions. However, you must do more to succeed. Use the interview to find out as much as possible about the company so you can decide if the job fits *your* requirements. Here are ten questions to help you gather the *intelligence* you need to decide if the company is a good bet.

1. **Why is this position open?** By asking this question, you will find out where the job fits within the company and the challenges of the position. Don't stop there. Ask why the previous employee left. If the position is new, determine its scope of responsibility.

2. **Could you tell me more about the company and this department?** If you are a finalist for the job, you should already know the basic facts about the company. While the interviewer's answers should confirm what you already know, it may reveal new information you can use to probe further.

3. **What are the company's immediate and long term goals?** Chances are you'll interview with more than one manager, so ask each this question and compare answers. Hearing different answers each time should raise flags.

4. **What attracted you to this company and what do you think are its strengths and weaknesses?** This is a subjective question but you will get specific input from someone working in the trenches. Other interviewers might give different answers, so consider the source and evaluate the responses. Remember, you are asking this question to get a personal view point.

5. **If I were offered and accepted this position, what is my growth potential?** This will tell you about advancement

opportunities (or lack thereof). It may also shed light on internal promotion policy. If your goal is to advance in your career, make sure the company will encourage it.

6. **What skills are most necessary to be successful in this company?** You have probably answered several questions by the time you ask your own, so you may know what skills are required. However, this question will tell you which are the "most necessary." Take advantage of this opportunity to let the employer know how you have applied these skills in the past and could do so again as their employee.

7. **Could someone with my background make the contribution you need in this position?** This subtle inquiry can help you learn how you are doing in the interview. You are not asking for the job but you are gaining immediate feedback regarding your application. If the employer mentions a skill you have not yet discussed, you still have time to do so while you are there.

8. **How many candidates are you interviewing for this position and have you been especially impressed by any of them?** Know something about your competition. The employer may divulge this information but you will never know unless you try. If another candidate's skills and accomplishments are mentioned, remind the interviewer of your equally appealing qualities.

9. **When do you expect to make a selection?** Never leave an interview without determining the next step. If the employer is not able to give you a definite answer, try to establish the next step yourself. Ask if you can call the next week to follow up (you should anyway). Nothing is more frustrating that leaving an interview without closure.

10. **Based upon our discussions, I am highly interested in this position because of x, y and z. Would you consider me for this position?** If you want the job, ask for it. Even

if it seems a little bold, you do not have anything to lose. Since a job opening often generates hundreds of applicants, if you have landed an interview, you have won half the battle.

Part II

Key Contacts For Targeting Your Job Search

9

Professional Organizations and Associations

T he following professional organizations and associations are important groups for networking with fellow professionals. Most groups have membership directories, hold regular meetings, and provide some career assistance to their members. Be sure to join the appropriate ones relevant to your professional interests, skills, and experience. They may play a central role in conducting an effective job search and finding the perfect job.

1st Military Intell Bn (ARS)
Mr. Michael J. Nash
31116 W. Angeline Court
St. Clair Shores, MI 48082-2416
810/296-3459 (H) or 810/447-3344 (W)
Fax 810/445-4098
cvnv24a@prodigy.com

4th Psyop Group
Richard Hofmann
5 Van Dyke Drive
Wilmington, DE 19809-3423
302/762-2115
hofmann@delmarva.com
76472.3414@compuserve.com

5th Military Intell Co, (Munich FRG '86/91)
Mr. Dwight C. Van Tassell
9 Crum Elbow Road
Hyde Park, NY 12538-2806
914/229-2473
xjxm64a@prodigy.com

502nd Military Intell Co, (2nd ACR Nuremberg Ger)
Mr. Stephen T. Peters
131 A Hatfield Street
Fort Huachuca, AZ 85613-1201
pete17@primenet.com *or* pete17@primenet.com

519th Military Intell Bn Assn
Mr. Gene Bateman
202 Hope Street
Oskaloosa, IA 52577-3041
515/673-6877
Newsletter
        Or
Mr. Manfred Groth
531 Santa Helena
San Antonio, TX 78232-2787
210/494-5124
LTC519@aol.com

75th Ranger Regiment Association
Treasurer
8688 Ruffian Lane
Newburgh, IN 47630

82nd Airborne Division Association—National
Mr. Manny De Jesus
NFCS P.O. Box 9308
Fayetteville, NC 28311-7694

Army Aviation Association of America
49 Richmondville Avenue
Westport, CT 06880-2000
203/226-8184, ext. 120
Fax: 203/222-9863
E-mail: aaaa@quad-a.org

Army Counter Intell Corps
Mr. Edwin L Simmons
5319 SW 15th Street
Topeka, KS 66604-2403
913/272-1609

Aerospace Industries Association
1250 Eye St., NW
Suite 1200
Washington, DC 20005-3924
202/371-8400
Fax: 202/371-8470
http://www.access.digex.net/~aia

Air Commando Association
2 David Street, Unit B
Fort Walton Beach, FL 32547
Tel/Fax 904/864-1953

Air Force Association
1501 Lee Highway
Arlington, VA 22209-1198
http://www.afa.org

Air Force Office of Special Investigations, Public Affairs Office
226 Duncan Avenue
Suite 2100
Bolling AFB, DC 20332-0001
202/767-5352

Air Force Sergeants Association
ATTN: Membership Department
P.O. Box 50
Temple Hills, MD 20757-0050
1/800/638-0595

American Defense Preparedness Association
2101 Wilson Blvd., Suite 400
Arlington, VA 22201-3061
703/522-1820
Fax: 703/522-1885

American Society for Industrial Security
1655 N. Fort Myer Drive, Suite 1200
Arlington, VA 22209-3198
703/522-5800
Fax: 703/276-3043

American Society of Naval Engineers (ASNE)
1452 Duke Street
Alexandria, VA 22314-3458
703/836-6727
Fax: 703/836-7491
E-mail: ecp@aplcomm.jhuapl.edu
http://www.jhuapl.edu/ASNE/

Armed Forces Communications and Electronics Association (AFCEA)
4400 Fair Lakes Court
Fairfax, VA 22033-3899
800/336-4583
Fax: 703/631-6100
E-mail: admin@afcea.org
http://www.afcea.org/

Association of Aviation Ordnancemen
C/O Secretary/Treasurer, LCDR Richard J. Grass USN Ret.
522 Edgehill Road, Apt 1B
Glenside, PA 19038-2521
215/887-5009
Fax: 215/887-5876
E-mail: byron@kingsnet.com

Association of Former Intelligence Officers
6723 Whittier Ave., Suite 303A
McLean, VA 22101-4533
703/790-0320
Fax: 703/790-0264

Association of Naval Aviation (ANA)
5205 Leesburg Pike, Suite 200
Falls Church, VA 22041
703/998-7733
Fax: 703/671-6052
E-mail: anahq@ix.netcom.com

Association of Naval Service Officers
Office of the National President
PO Box 10951
Arlington, VA 22203-1951
703/696-4877
Fax: 703/696-2787

Association of Old Crows (AOC)
The AOC Building
1000 North Payne Street
Alexandria, VA 22314-1696
703/549-1600
Fax: 703/549-2589

Business Espionage Controls &
Countermeasures Association (BECCA)
P.O. Box 260
Ft. Washington, MD 20749
301/292-6430
Fax: 301/292-4635

CID Agents Association
CIDAA Membership Chairman
3613 Concord Court
Augusta, GA 30906

Council of Defense & Space Industry Associations (CODSIA)
1250 Eye Street, NW
Suite 1100
Washington, DC 20005
202/371-8414
Fax: 202/371-8470

Counter Intell Corps Assn (National)
Mr. Joseph B. Quatman
327 N Elizabeth Street
Lima, OH 45801-4304
419/225-2261

Federal Law Enforcement Officers Association
P.O. Box 508
East Northport, NY 11731-0472
http://fleoa.org/index.html

Fleet Reserve Association Headquarters
125 N. West Street
Alexandria, VA 22314-2754
703/683-1400
E-mail: news-fra@fra.org
http://www.cais.net/fra/

Force Reconnaissance Association
3784-B Mission Avenue
Suite 1775
Oceanside, CA 92054
Executive Director Gary Marte
619/439-8633

Former Intell Officer, Assn of
Mr. John F. Blake
6723 Whittier Ave.
Suite 303A
McLean, VA 22101-4533
703/790-0320

Freedom Through Vigilance Association
7323 Highway 90 West
Suite 16
San Antonio, TX 78227

**International Association of Counterterrorism &
Security Professionals (IACSP)**
P.O. Box 10265
Arlington, VA 22210
Fax: 703/243-1197
http://www.worldonline.net/securitynet/IACSP/

**International Association of Law Enforcement
Intelligence Analysts**
Ms. Debbie Ansman, President
Washington Area Chapter
IALEIA c/o Financial Intelligence Center
2070 Chainbridge Road
Vienna, VA 22182
703/905-3562 or Fax: 703/905-3680

**International Association of
Personal Protection Specialists**
IAPPS World Headquarters
1190 Homestead Road
Santa Clara, CA 95050
E-mail: info@iapps.org
http://www.iapps.org

International Chief Petty Officers Association
P.O. Box 12328
Las Vegas, NV 89112-0328
800/494-2762
E-mail: devem42a@prodigy.com
http://members.aol.com/icpoa/inex.html

Marine Corps Aviation Reconnaissance Association
P.O. Box 2138
Lake Havasu City, AZ 86405-2138

Marine Corps Counterintelligence Association
P.O. Box 3029
Virginia Beach, VA 23454
President John McMakin
804/481-6163

Marine Corps Cryptologic Association
P.O. Drawer E
Woodbridge, VA 22194

Marine Corps Intelligence Association, Inc.
P.O. Box 1028
Quantico, VA 22134
E-mail: kdpi@aol.com

Marine Corps League
National Headquarters
PO Box 3070
Merrifield, VA 22116-3070
703/207-9588
http://www.cris.com/~marine1/MCL.htm

Military Intelligence Corps Association
P.O. Box 13020
Fort Huachuca, AZ 85670-3020
Fax: 520/803-9000
http://www.primenet.com/~usamica/index.html
MICA President John H. Black
502/378-0209
103525.1562@compuserve.com

Mine Warfare Association
P.O. Box 185
Newington, VA 22122-0185
E-mail: amb@minwara.org
http://www.minwara.org/

National Military Intelligence Association
Editor in Chief
P.O. Box 6712
Falls Church, VA 22040
703/824-3211
Fax: 703/824-0334
E-Mail: jonkers@betac.com

National Security Industrial Association (NSIA)
1025 Connecticut Avenue NW, Suite 300
Washington, DC 20036-5405
202/775-1440
Fax: 202/775-1309

Naval Cryptologic Veterans Association
4809 Listra Road
Rockville, MD 20853
800/872-6282
Fax: 301/933-7041

Navy Enlisted Reserve Association
6703 Farragut Avenue
Falls Church, VA 22042-2189
800/776-9020
Fax: 703/534-3617
E-mail: wjpelka@thefuture.net

Naval Helicopter Association
P.O. Box 180460
Coronado, CA 92178-0460
619/435-7139
Fax: 619/435-7354
E-mail: rotorrev@gnn.com
http://dubhe.cc.nps.navy.mil/~nha/

Naval Intelligence Foundation
P.O. Box 10422
McLean, VA 22102-8422

Naval Intelligence Professionals, Inc.
NIP Journal Editor
P.O. Box 9324
McLean, VA 22102-0324
703/437-7487
E-mail: 76513.15@compuserve.com
http://www.oss.net/oss/nip

Naval Reserve Association
1619 King Street
Alexandria, VA 22314
703 548 5800
Fax: 703/683-3647
http://www.navy-reserve.org/index.html

Navy League of the United States
2300 Wilson Boulevard
Arlington, VA 22201
800/356-5760
E-mail: mail@navyleague.org
http://www.navyleague.org/

Operations Security Professional Society
9200 Centerway Road
Gaithersburg, MD 20879
301/840-6770 or Fax: 301/840-8502
E-Mail: zhi@tiac.com
http://www.opsec.org

OV-1 Mohawk Association
1360 Keenan Way
San Jose, CA 95125
888/7Mohawk
http://www.ov-1mohawk.org/

Society of Competitive Intelligence Professionals
1700 Diagonal Road, Suite 520
Alexandria, VA 22314
703/739-0696 or Fax: 703/739-2524
E-mail: scip@dc.infi.net
http://www.scip.org

Society of Naval Architects and Marine Engineers
601 Pavonia Avenue
Jersey City, NJ 07306
201/798-4800
Fax: 201/798-4975
E-mail: webmaster@www.sname.org
http://www.sname.org/

Special Forces Association
P.O. Box 41436
Fayetteville, NC 28309-1436
910/485-5433
Fax: 910/485-1041
E-mail: sfahq@sfahq.org
http://www.sfahq.org

Surface Navy Association
205 Burtonwood Drive
Alexandria, VA 22307
800/NAVYUSA
E-mail: national@navysna.org
http://www.cais.net/sna/

Tailhook Association
9696 Businesspark Avenue
San Diego, CA 92131-1643
619/689-9227
E-mail: thookassn@aol.com
http://www.Tailhook.org/

The Retired Enlisted Association
National Headquarters
1111 S. Abilene Court
Aurora, CO 80012
800/338-9337
Fax: 303/752-0835
E-mail: treahq@trea.org
http://www.trea.org

UDT-SEAL Association
P.O. Box 5365
Virginia Beach, VA 23455
804/363-7490
Fax: 804/481-2113
E-Mail: udtseal@pinn.net

US Air Force Air Weather Association
1879 Cole Road
Aromas, CA 95004

US Army Ranger Association, Inc.
P.O. Box 52126
Ft. Benning, GA 31995-2126
706/323-6811
E-mail: asilsby@ac.america.net
http://www.ranger.org/~ranger/usara/usara.htm

World EOD Foundation
C/O OSPREY USA
1825 Eye Street, Suite 400
Washington, DC 20006
202/429-6836

10

Professional and Community Publications

Familiarize yourself with what's going on in your professional field as well as survey major employers relevant to your interests, skills, and experience by examining the following publications.

Air Chronicles
http://www.cdsar.af.mil/air-chronicles.html

Airman Magazine
GPO Superintendent of Documents
Box 371954
Pittsburgh, PA 15250-7954

Army Aviation Magazine
49 Richmondville Avenue
Westport, CT 06880-2000
203/226-8184
fax: 203/222-9863
E-mail: aaaa@quad-a.org

Armed Forces Journal International
2000 L Street, NW, Suite 520
Washington, DC 20036-4912
202/296-0450
Fax: 202/296-5727
http:\\www.afji.com

Combat Craft
P.O Box 268
Boston, MA 02117-0268
Steve Trimmer, Tech Editor
757/631-0607 or Fax: 757/631-0607
www.combat-craft.com

CovertAction Quarterly
Dept. MFW
1500 Massachusetts Ave., NW, Suite 732
Washington, DC 20005
Fax: 202/331-9751

Cryptolog
Naval Cryptologic Veterans Association
4809 Listra Road
Rockville, MD 20853-3124

Defense Daily
1111 North 19th Street, Suite 503
Arlington, VA 22209
703/522-5655

Defense News
Army Times Publishing Co.
6883 Commercial Dr.
Springfield, VA 22159-0400

Federal Career Opportunities
Federal Research Service, Inc.
243 Church Street, Suite 200
Vienna, VA 22180-4434
703/281-0200 or Fax: 703/281-7639
E-mail: info@fedjobs.com
http://www.fedjobs.com

High Technology Careers Magazine
4701 Patrick Henry Drive
Suite 1901
Santa Clara, CA 95054

The Inscom Journal
U.S. Army Intelligence and Security Command
Ft. Belvoir, VA
703/806-6325/6843
Fax: 703/806-5647

Intelligence Online
Indigo Publications
10 Rue du Sentier
75002 Paris - France
http://www.indigo-net.com/intel.html

Intelligence Watch Report (Online)
Tempest Co.
P.O. Box 15095
Boston, MA 02215
617/266-5637
Fax: 617/266-7680
E-mail: tempest@.tiac.net
IntelWeb: http://www.awpi.com/intelweb
Recommended Book Listing: http://awpi.com/intelweb/iwr/books.html

**International Journal of Intelligence
and Counter Intelligence**
Intel Publishing Group, Inc.
Box 188
Stroudsburg, PA 18360

**The Journal of Counterterrorism and
Security International**
P.O. Box 10265
Arlington, VA 22210
703/243-0993
Fax: 703/243-1197
http://www.securitynet.net

Military Intelligence Professional Bulletin
Commander, USAIC&FH
Attn: ATZS-TDL-B
Ft. Huachuca, AZ 85613-6000
520/538-1005

National Defense
2101 Wilson Blvd.
Suite 400
Arlington, VA 22201

Naval Proceedings
US Naval Institute
2062 General Highway
Annapolis, MD 21401
Fax: 410/224-2406

Security Management Magazine
American Society For Industrial Security
1655 North Fort Meyer Dr.
Suite 1200
Arlington, VA 22209-9958
703/522-5800
Fax: 703/243-4954

Signal (AFCEA)
4400 Fair Lakes Court
Fairfax, VA 22033
800/336-4583 (in USA)
Fax: 703/631-6160
E-mail: signal@us.net

11

Community Addresses, Phone Numbers and Internet Sites

Members of our community are associated with the following organizations that specialize in special operations and intelligence. Many individuals have worked for more than one of these organizations. You may want to consider opportunities with these groups.

Advanced Research Projects Agency (ARPA)
3701 North Fairfax Drive
Arlington, VA 22203-1714
703/696-2442
Fax: 703/696-2208

Air Force Office of Special Investigations
Public Affairs Office
226 Duncan Avenue
Suite 2100
Bolling AFB, DC 20332-0001
202/767-5352

Bureau of Alcohol, Tobacco and Firearms
650 Massachusetts Avenue, NW
Washington, DC 20005
BATF Personnel Hotline: 202/927-8423
E-mail: persdiv@atfhg.atf.treas.gov

Bureau of Prisons
HOLC Building, Room 161
Washington, DC 20534
Personnel: 202/307-1304
Vacancies: 202/514-6388

Center for Defense Information
1500 Massachusetts Avenue, N.W.
Washington, DC 20005
202/862-0700
Fax: 202/862-0708

Center For Remote Sensing
Boston University
725 Commonwealth Avenue
Boston, MA 02215
617/353-9709
Fax: 617/353-3200

Central Intelligence Agency
Office of Personnel
Washington, DC 20505
Vacancies: 800/562-7242
http://www.odci.gov/cia

Chemical Biological Defense Agency
Aberdeen Proving Ground, MD 21010-5423
410/671-4345
Fax: 410/671-5297

CIA Recruitment Division
Send resume and cover letter to:
P.O. Box 12727
Arlington, VA 22209-8727
Voice Reference System: 800/562-7242

Critical Intervention Services, Inc.
1265 S. Missouri Avenue
Clearwater, FL 34616
813/461-9417
Fax: 813/449-1269
E-mail: cis@webcom.com
http://www.webcom.com/cis/welcome.html

Commander 111th MI Bde
Attn: ATZS-TPS
Ft. Huachuca, AZ 85613-6000

Commander
304th Military Intelligence Battalion
Attn: ATZS-TPP
Ft. Huachuca, AZ 85613-6000
520/533-5994
Fax: 520/533-2607

Commander
525th MI BDE
Ft. Bragg, NC
910/396-6574/5266/9301

CDR, PERSCOM
Attn: TAPC-OPF-MI
200 Stovall St.
Alexandria, VA 22332-0415

Defense Advanced Research Projects Administration
3701 North Fairfax Drive
Arlington, VA 22203-1714
202/545-7000
E-mail: kpulzone@darpa.mil

Defense Information Systems Agency
Civilian Personnel Office
Attn: D111, Bldg. 2, Room 201
701 S. Courthouse Road
Arlington, VA 22204-2199
703/607-4400 or DSN 327-4400
Job Vacancies: 703/607-4424 or DSN 327-4424

Defense Intelligence Agency (DIA)
200 MacDill Blvd.
Civilian Personnel Division (DAH-2)
Washington, DC 20340-5100
703/695-7353
www.dia.mil

Civilian Personnel Office
202/231-4311
DSN 428-4311
Recruitment: 202/907-1339 (8:00 - 4:30 PM)

Vacancy Announcement System
800/526-4629 or 703/907-1710
DSN 283-1710

Defense Investigative Service
Resources Directorate
1340 Braddock Place
Alexandria, VA 22314
Personnel: 703/325-6186

Defense Logistics Agency
Staff Director Civilian Personnel
Cameron Station
Alexandria, VA 22304-6100
703/274-6019
Personnel: 703/274-7088
Vacancies: 703/274-7372

Defense Mapping Agency
8613 Lee Highway
Fairfax, VA 22031-2137
703/285-9374
Personnel: 703/285-9148
Recruitment: 800/526-3379

Defense Nuclear Agency (DNA)
6801 Telegraph Road
Alexandria, VA 22310-3398
703/325-7004
202/545-6700

Department of The Air Force
NCR-SPTGDPC, CPO 1100
The Pentagon
Room 5E871
Washington, DC 20330
Personnel: 703/695-5206
Vacancies: 703/693-6550

Department of The Army
Hoffman CPAC, Building II
Room 1S39
200 Stovall St.
ATTN: ANCP-HPR
Alexandria, VA 22332-0800
Personnel: 703/325-8840
Vacancies: 703/325-8841

Department of The Navy
National Maritime Intelligence Center
Hotline: 301/669-4000

Department of the Navy
Human Resources Office
Washington Navy Yard, Building 200
11th & M Street., SE
Washington, DC 20374
Personnel: 202/433-5370
Vacancies: 202/433-4931

Department of the Navy
Secretariat/Headquarters
Human Resources Office
Under Secretary of the Navy
2211 Jefferson Davis Highway
Crystal Plaza 5, Room 236
Arlington, VA 22244-5101
Personnel: 703/602-2195

Drug Enforcement Administration
700 Army-Navy Drive
Arlington, VA 22202
Personnel: 202/307-4055
Special Agent Recruitment: 202/307-4100

Executive Security International (ESI)
Gun Bun Barrel Square
2128 Railroad Ave. , Dept W
Rifle, CO 81650
800/874-0888
E-mail: duggam@esi-lifeforce.com
http://www.esi-lifeforce.com

Federal Aviation Administration
800 Independence Ave., SW
Washington, DC 20591
Personnel: 202/267-8008
Vacancies: 202/267-8007

Federal Bureau of Investigation
Personnel Office, JEH Building
10th St. & Pennsylvania Ave., NW
Room 6647
Washington, DC 20571
Personnel: 202/324-4991
Vacancies: 202/324-3674

Federal Communications Commission
1919 M St., NW
Room 216
Washington, DC 20554
Personnel: 202/418-0130
Vacancies: 202/418-0101

Federal Emergency Management Agency
500 C Street, SW
Room 816
Washington, DC 20472
Vacancies: 202/646-3244

Federal Law Enforcement Training Center
US Department of Treasury, DC
202/927-8940
Civilian Personnel Office, Glynco, GA
912/267-2288

Federal Protective Service
18th & F Streets, NW
Washington, DC 20405
http://gsa.gov/pbs/fps/fps.htm

Goddard Space Flight Center
Employment Hotline: 301/286-5326
301/286-7918

HQ National Air Intelligence Center
Public Affairs
Wright-Patterson AFB, OH 45433-5605
937/257-6487

Immigration and Naturalization Service
Personnel and Training
CAB Building, Room 2038
425 I St., NW
Washington, DC 20536
Personnel: 202/514-2530
Vacancies: 202/514-4301

Institute for Defense Analysis (IDA)
1801 N. Beauregard Street
Alexandria, VA 22311-1772
703/845-2000 or Fax: 703/845-2569

Jane's Information Group
1340 Braddock Place, Suite 300
Alexandria, VA 22314
800/824-0768 or 703/683-3700
Fax: 800/836-0297 or 703/836-1593
E-mail: iwr@janes.com
http://www.awpi.com/intelweb

Jet Propulsion Laboratory, NASA (JPL)
4800 Oak Grove Drive
Pasadena, CA 91109
818/354-4321 or Fax: 818/354-2204

Joint Military Intelligence College
Washington, DC 20340-5100
202/373-3344 or Fax: 202/373-4977

Marine Corps Combat Development Command
Civilian Personnel Department
Quantico, VA 22134
Personnel: 703/640-2048

Massachusetts Institute of Technology,
Department of Ocean Engineering
77 Massachusetts Ave., Room 5-228
Cambridge, MA 02139
617/253-4330 or Fax: 617/253-8125
E-mail: ocean-www@mit.edu
http://web.mit.edu/ocean/www/

National Aeronautics and Space Administration
300 E St., SW
Washington, DC 20546
Personnel: 202/358-1546

National Ground Intelligence Center
220 7th Street, NE
Charlottesville, VA 22902-5396

National Oceanic and Atmospheric Administration
Career Resource Center
1335 East-West Highway, Room 2262
Silver Spring, MD 20910
Personnel: 301/713-0677 or Vacancies: 301/713-1377
E-mail: opca@esdim.noaa.gov
http://www.noaa.gov/

National Reconnaissance Office
Office of Corporate Communications
14675 Lee Road
Chantilly, VA 20151-1715
703/808-1198 or Fax: 703/808-1171

National Security Agency
Civilian Employment Office
Mail resume, college transcripts and DD 214 to:
National Security Agency
Attn.: M3212
Ft Meade, MD 20755-6000
410/859-6444 Civilian Employment Office voice recording

National Security Industrial Association (NSIA)
1025 Connecticut Avenue, NW, Suite 300
Washington, DC 20036-5405
202/775-1440
Fax: 202/775-1309

National Technical Information Service
Technology Administration
U.S. Department of Commerce
Springfield, VA 22161
403/487-4650
Fax: 703/321-8547

Naval Air Systems Command HQ
 (NAVAIRSYSCOM)
Jefferson Plaza Building 1
Washington, DC 20361-0001
202/692-2260

Naval Criminal Investigative Service Headquarters
NCIS Headquarters
Washington Navy Yard
Building 111
901 M Street, SE
Washington, DC 20388
202/763-3780

> **Washington Field Office**
> Washington Navy Yard
> Building 200
> Washington, DC 20374
> 202/433-3858

Naval Education and Training Center (NETC)
Newport, RI 02841
401/841-3538
Fax: 401/841-2655

Naval Education & Training Program Management
Support Activity (NETPMSA)
6490 Saufley Field Road
Pensacola, FL 32509-5237

Naval Facilities Engineering Command
Headquarters (NAVFACENGCOM)
Jefferson Plaza Building 1
Washington, DC 20361-0001
Tel: 202/692-2260

Naval Legal Service Command
Hoffman Building 2
200 Stovall St.
Alexandria, VA
Tel: 703/325-9820

Naval Oceanographic Office (NAVOCEANO)
1002 Balch Boulevard
Stennis Space Center, MS 39522-5001
601/688-4367
Fax: 601/688-4191

Naval Postgraduate School
1 University Circle
Monterey, CA 93943-5001
202/767-3200
E-mail: webmaster@nps.navy.mil
http://www.nps.navy.mil/

Naval Research Laboratory
Human Resources Office
Code 1810
4555 Overlook Ave., SW
Washington, DC 20375-5324
Personnel: 202/767-3030

Naval Security Group Command
3801 Nebraska Avenue, NW
Washington, DC
202/282-0444

Naval Space Command HQ
Dahlgren, VA 22448-5300
703/663-6100

Naval Surface Warfare Center
Carderrock Division, Code 32
Human Resources Office
Bethesda, MD 20084-5000
Personnel: 301/227-4160
Vacancies: 301/227-2828

Naval Undersea Warfare Center (NUWC)
Newport, RI 02841-1708
401/841-3611
Fax: 401/841-3035

Office of Export Enforcement, Intelligence Division
Room 4520, 14th Street and Constitution Avenue, N.W.
U.S. Department of Commerce
Washington, DC 20230
202/482-1208
Fax: 202/482-0964

Office of Naval Research
Ballston Tower 1
800 North Quincy Street
Arlington, VA 22217-5660
703/696-5031
http://www.onr.navy.mil/onr

Polaris Missile Facility ATL/NAD
Charleston, SC
803/764-4114 or Fax: 803/764-4074

Profiles Threat Counter Measures Group
19672 Stevens Creek Blvd., Suite 215
Cupertino, CA 95014
408/865-0951 or Fax: 408/273-6082
E-mail: profiles@profiles-threat.com

Scotti School
10 High Street, Suite 15
Medford, MA 02155
800/343-0046 or 781/395-9156
Fax: 781/391-8252
E-mail: scotti@ssdd.com
http://www.ssdd.com

Trident Training Facility Bangor
2000 Thresher Avenue
Silverdale, WA 98315-2000
206/396-4945

United States Coast Guard
2100 Second Street, SW
Washington, DC 20593
202/267-2229
E-mail: uscgweb@mailstorm.dot.gov
http://www.dot.gov/dotinfo/uscg/welcome.html

US Customs Service
2120 L St., NW, 6th Floor
Washington, DC 20037
Personnel: 202/634-5270
General Information: 202/927-6724

US Department of Energy
Office of Personnel
HQ, Personnel Services Division, AD-52
1000 Independence Ave., SW
Washington, DC 20585
Vacancies: 202/586-4333

US Department of Justice
12th & Pennsylvania Ave., NW
Washington, DC 20530
Personnel: 202/514-6813
Vacancies: 202/514-6818

US Department of Justice
National Drug Intelligence Center
8201 Greensboro Dr., Suite 1001
McLean, VA 22102
703/556-8970
Employment Hotline Extension 258

US Department of State
Employment Information Office
22nd & D St., NW
Room 2819
Washington, DC 20520

Civil Service Recruitment Branch
202/647-7252
Hotline: 202/647-7284

Foreign Service Recruitment Division
P.O. Box 9317
Arlington, VA 22219
Vacancies: 703/875-7490

US Department of Transportation
DOT Connection M 18.1
400 7th St., SW
Room 9113
Washington, DC 20590
Personnel: 202/366-9391
Vacancies: 202/366-9397

US Information Agency
301 4th St., SW
Room 518
Washington, DC 20547
Personnel: 202/619-4659
Vacancies: 202/619-4539

US Marshall Service
Personnel Office
Suite 890
600 Army Navy Drive
Arlington, VA 22202
Personnel: 202/307-9600

US Naval Academy
121 Blake Road
Annapolis, MD 21402-5000
410/293-2291
Fax: 410/293-3133

US Naval Diving & Salvage Training Center
Panama City, FL 32407-5002
904/234-4651
Fax: 904/235-5253

US Naval Institute
2062 Generals Highway
Annapolis, MD 21401
800/233-8764
Fax: 410/224-2406
E-mail: webmaster@usni.org
http://www.usni.org/

US Naval War College
686 Cushing Road
Newport, RI 02841-1207
401/841-3089
Fax: 401/841-3804

US Nuclear Regulatory Commission
Office of Human Resources
Washington, DC 20555-0001

US Special Operations Command
Public Affairs Office
MacDill AFB, FL 33608-6001
813/828-4604

US Treasury Department
United States Secret Service
Civilian Personnel Office: 202/435-5800

US Treasury Department
Internal Revenue Service
1111 Constitution Ave., NW
Room 1034
Washington, DC 20224
Personnel/Vacancies: 202/622-6340

Voice of America
330 Independence Ave., SW
Room 1543
Washington, DC 20547
Personnel: 202/619-3117
Vacancies: 202/619-0909

12

Federal Job Information Touch Screen Computers

Located throughout the nation, Federal Job Information Touch Screen Computers provide current worldwide Federal job opportunities, on-line information, and the ability to request application packages. You will find a Touch Screen computer at the following locations:

Alabama: Huntsville
520 Wynn Dr., NW

Alaska: Anchorage
Federal Bldg.,
222 W. 7th Ave.
Rm. 156

Arizona: Phoenix
VA Medical Center,
650 E. Indian School Rd.,
Bldg. 21, Rm. 141

Arkansas: Little Rock
Federal Bldg., 700 W. Capitol
1st Floor Lobby

California: Sacramento
1029 J St., Rm. 202

Colorado: Denver
12345 W. Alameda Pkwy.
Room 101
Lakewood

Connecticut: Hartford
Federal Bldg.
450 Main St., Rm. 133

District of Columbia:
Washington, DC
Theodore Roosevelt Federal Bldg
1900 E St., NW, Rm. 1416

Florida: Miami
Downtown Jobs and Benefits
   Center
Florida Job Service Center
401 NW, 2nd Ave., Ste N-214

Florida: Orlando
Florida Job Service Center
1001 Executive Center Dr.
First Floor

Georgia: Atlanta
Richard B. Russell Federal Bldg.
Main Lobby, Plaza Level
75 Spring St., SW

Hawaii: Honolulu
Federal Bldg., Rm. 5316
300 Ala Moana Blvd.

Hawaii: Fort Shafter
Department of Army
Army Civilian Personnel Office
Army Garrison, Bldg. T-1500

Illinois: Chicago
77 West Jackson Blvd.
1st Floor Lobby

Indiana: Indianapolis
Minton-Capehart Fed. Bldg.
575 N. Pennsylvania St., Rm. 339

Louisiana: New Orleans
Federal Bldg.
423 Canal St.
1st Floor Lobby

Maine: Augusta
Federal Office Bldg.
40 Western Ave.

Maryland: Baltimore
George H. Fallon Bldg.
Lombard St. & Hopkins Plaza
Lobby

Massachusetts: Boston
Thomas P. O'Neill, Jr. Federal
   Bldg.
10 Causeway St.
2nd Floor

Michigan: Detroit
477 Michigan Ave.
Rm. 565

Minnesota: Twin Cities
Bishop Henry Whipple Federal
   Bldg.
1 Federal Drive
Rm. 501
Ft. Snelling

Missouri: Kansas City
Federal Bldg.
601 E. 12th St.
Rm. 134

New Hampshire: Portsmouth
Thomas McIntyre Federal Bldg.
80 Daniel St.
1st Floor Lobby

New Jersey: Newark
Peter J. Rodino Federal Bldg.
970 Broad St.
2nd Floor

New Mexico: Albuquerque
New Mexico State Job Service
501 Mountain Rd.
Lobby

New York: Albany
Leo W. O'Brian Federal Bldg.
Clinton Ave. & North Pearl
Basement Level

New York: Buffalo
Thaddeus T. Dulski Federal Bldg.
111 West Huron St.
9th Floor

New York: New York City
Jacob K. Javits Federal Bldg.
26 Federal Plaza
Lobby

New York: New York City
290 Broadway
Lobby

New York: Syracuse
James M. Hanley Federal Bldg.
100 S. Clinton St.

Ohio: Dayton
Federal Bldg.
200 W. 2nd St.
Rm. 509

Oklahoma: Oklahoma City
Career Connection Center
7401 NE, 23rd St.

Oregon: Portland
Federal Bldg.
Rm. 376
1220 SW Third Ave.

Pennsylvania: Harrisburg
Federal Bldg.
228 Walnut St.
Rm. 168

Pennsylvania: Philadelphia
William J. Green, Jr. Federal
  Bldg.
600 Arch St.

Pennsylvania: Pittsburgh
Federal Bldg.
1000 Liberty Ave.
1st Floor

Pennsylvania: Reading
Reading Postal Service
2100 N. 13th St.

Puerto Rico: San Juan
US Federal Bldg.
150 Carlos Chardon Ave.
Rm. 328

Rhode Island: Providence
380 Westminster
Mall Lobby

Tennessee: Memphis
Naval Air Station Memphis
Transition Assistance Center
7800 3rd Ave.
Bldg. South 239
Millington

Texas: Dallas
Federal Bldg.
1st Floor Lobby
1100 Commerce St.

Texas: El Paso
Federal Bldg.
700 East San Antonio St.
Lobby

Texas: Houston
Mickey Leland Federal Bldg.
1919 Smith St.
1st Floor Lobby

Texas: San Antonio
Federal Bldg.
1st Floor Lobby
727 East Durango

Utah: Salt Lake City
Utah State Job Service
720 South 2nd East

Vermont: Burlington
Federal Bldg.
11 Elmwood Ave.
1st Floor Lobby

Virginia: Norfolk
Federal Bldg.
200 Granby St.

Washington: Seattle
Federal Bldg.
915 Second Ave.
Rm. 110

13

Office of Personnel Management (OPM) Employment Service Offices

The following regional branches of the Office of Personnel Management provide information on the Federal application process. Contact the one nearest you for application forms and other related information, including information on Federal agencies within each region.

Office of Personnel Management (Central Office)
Theodore Roosevelt Building
1900 E Street, NW
Washington, DC 20415-0001
202/606-2700
Covers: Washington, DC, Virginia and Maryland

Atlanta Service Center
Richard B. Russell Federal Building
75 Spring Street SW
Suite 940
Atlanta, GA 30303-3109
404/331-4588
Covers: Florida and Georgia

Chicago Service Center
John C. Kuczynski Federal Building - DPN 30-3
230 South Dearborn Street
Chicago, IL 60604-1687
312/353-6234
Covers: Illinois, Iowa and Wisconsin

Dayton Service Center
US Courthouse and Federal Building
200 West 2nd Street, Room 507
Dayton, OH 45402-0001
513/225-2576
Covers: Indiana, Kentucky, Southern Ohio and West Virginia

Denver Service Center
12345 West Alameda Parkway
P.O. Box 25167
Denver, CO 80225-0001
303/969-6931
Covers: Arizona, Colorado, Montana, New Mexico, Texas, Utah and
Wyoming

Detroit Service Center
477 Michigan Avenue, Room 594
Detroit, MI 48226-2574
313/226-7522
Covers: Indiana, Kentucky, Michigan and Northern Ohio

Honolulu Service Center
300 Ala Moana Boulevard
Box 50028
Honolulu, HI 96850-0001
808/541-2795
Covers: Alaska, Hawaii and Pacific Overseas

Huntsville Service Center
520 Wynn Drive, NW
Huntsville, AL 35816-3426
205/837-1271
Covers: Arkansas, Alabama, Mississippi and Tennessee

Kansas City Service Center
601 East 12th Street, Room 301
Kansas City, MO 64106-2826
816/426-5705
Covers: Illinois, Iowa, Kansas, Missouri and Nebraska

Norfolk Service Center
Federal Building
200 Granby Street, Room 500
Norfolk, VA 23510-1886
804/441-3373
Covers: Virginia

Philadelphia Service Center
William J. Green, Jr. Federal Building
600 Arch Street, Room 3256
Philadelphia, PA 19106-1596
215/597-7670
Covers: Connecticut, Delaware, Maine, Massachusetts, New Hampshire,
New Jersey, New York, Pennsylvania, Rhode Island and Vermont.

Raleigh Service Center
4407 Bland Road, Suite 2200
Raleigh, NC 27609-6296
919/790-2817
Covers: North Carolina and South Carolina

14

Key Web Sites

It's very difficult to keep Web addresses current and accurate given the rapid changes taking place on the Internet these days. Many organizations change their Web addresses or create new sites. If any of the following Web addresses are out of date, which some may be, please use the various search engines to find their new address.

Department of Labor/OPM	*http://safetynet.doleta.gov*
Federal Times	*http://www.federaltimes.com*
CIA	*http://www.odci.gov/cia*
NOAA	*http://www.noaa.gov/noaa-image-home.html*
NSA	*http://www.nsa.gov:8080/*
BATF	*http://www.atf.treas.gov*
The Defense Department	*http://www.dtic.mil/defenselink*
Navy	*http://www.navy.mil*
Air Force	*http://www.af.mil/*
Department of Energy	*http://www.doe.gov*
ADPA	*http://www.adpansia.org*
FAS	*http://www.fas.org*
ARPA	*http://www.arpa.mil*
SPAWAR	*http://dolomite.spawar.navy.mil/spawar/welcome.page*
DISA	*http://www.disa.mil*
HQ Air Force	*http://www.hq.af.mil*

DLA	*http://www.dla.mil*
NIMA	*http://www.nima.mil*
US Army	*http://www.army.mil*
FBI	*http://www.fbi.gov*
DEA	*http://www.usdoj.gov/dea*
USIS	*http://www.usia.gov*
FAA	*http://www.faa.gov*
FEMA	*http://www.fema.gov*
DOJ	*us http://usdoj.gov*
USAIC/Schoolhouse	*http://huachuca-usaic.army.mil/*
OSS	*http://www.oss.net/oss/*
434TH MI Det (Strat)	*http://www.eajardines.com/434mid.html*
NRO	*http://www.odci.gov/ic/usic/nro.html*
DOS Foreign Affairs Network	*http://dosfan.lib.uic.edu/*
NMIA	*http://www.cache.net/NMIA*
Center for Defense Information	*http://www.cdi.org*
National Security Institute	*http://nsi.org*
NACIC	*http://www.awpi.com/IntelWeb/US/NCC/index.html*
DOE National Labs	*http://www.esd.ornl.gov/doe-labs/doe-labs.html*
US Department of State	*http://www.state.gov*
Department of the Treasury	*http://www.ustreas.gov*
Operations Security Prof. Society	*http://www.oss.net/ops*
Journal Of Elec. Defense (Old Crows)	*http://www.jedefense.com/jed.html*
Naval Reserve Association Job & Talent Bank	
	http://www.navy-reserve.org/index.html
U. S. Office of Personnel Management	*http://www.usajobs.opm.gov*
11 MSS/DPC CPO (Bolling)	*http://www.bolling.af.mil/civper/mssdpc.htm*
U.S. Secret Service	*http://www.ustreas.gov/treasury/bureaus/usss/usss.html*
Federal Bureau of Prisons	*http://gopher.usdoj.gov/bureaus/bop.html*
Investigator & Law Enforcement Offices	*http://www.usdog.gov/bureaus/*
USA Criminal Investigation Command	
	http://www.belvoir.army.mil/cidc/index.htm
United States Marshals Service	*http://usdoj.gov/marshals/*
Headquarters Air Combat Command	*http://www.acc.af.mil/*
HQ Air Force Space Command	
	http://www.spacecom.af.mil/hqafspc/index.htm
Ballistic Missile Defense Organization	
	http://www.acq.osd.mil/bmdo/bmdolink/html
Defense Technical Information Center	*http://www.dtic.dla.mil*
Naval Surface Warfare Center	*http://www.nswses.navy.mil*
US Air Force Academy	*http://www.usafa.af.mil*
Army High Performance Computing Center	*http://www.arc.umn.edu*
US DoD Defense Laboratory Community	*http://www.dtic.dla.mil:80/lablink/*
Naval Research Laboratory	*http://www.nrl.navy.mil*
USAF Rome Laboratory	*http://www.rl.af.mil/Locator/*

US Customs Service
 http://www.ustreas.gov/treasury/bureaus/customs/customs.html
The Police Officer's Internet Directory   *http://www.Officer.com*
Financial Crimes Enforcement Network
 http://www.ustreas.gov/treasury/bureaus/fincen/
Federal Law Enforcement Training Center
 http://www.ustreas.gov/treasury/bureaus/fletc/
Naval Air Warfare Center Weapons Division
 http://www.chinalake.navy.mil/oldNAWCWPNSHome.html

Miscellaneous

http://www.tscm.com
http://www.fedworld.gov
http://www.well.com/conf/war/iwsites.html
http://www.awpi.com:80/IntelWeb/
http://www.onestep.com:80/milnet
http://www.infomanage.com/international/intelligence/default.html
http://www.sagal.com/ajax/
http://www.fedcenter.com

General Career Resources

http://www.clearinghouse.net/
http://www.hoovers.com/
http://www.americasemployers.com/
http://www.careermosaic.com/
http://www.careerbuilder.com
http://www.cweb.com/
http://www.ep.com/h/reg/html
http://www.clickit.com/touch/execunet/execunet.html
http://www.nationjob.com
http://www.careermag.com/careermag/index.html
http://www.occ.com
http://www.conquest-prod.com/jobnetwrk/main2.html
http://www.monster.com
http://www.ceweekly.wa.com/contract/index.html
http://www.espan.com
http://www.intellimatch.com
http://www.jobweb.org
http://www.jobdirect.com
http://www.interbiznet.com
http://www.lib.umich.edu/chdocs/employment/
http://www.161.31.2.29/job.html
http://www.rescomp.stanford.edu/jobs/

http://www.rpi.edu/dept/cdc/metaindex.html
http://www.jobtrak.com/
http://www.yahoo.com/business/employment/jobs/
http://www.umn.edu/apn
http://www.jobbankusa.com/
http://www.careersite.com/
http://www.gis.umn.edu/rsgisinfo/jobs.html
http://nstaff.sunyerie.edu/home/crcn/index.htm
http://www2.monster.com:80/
http://www.career.com/
http://www.jobweb.com/
http://www.jobsource.com/
http://www.webcom.com/~career/
http://www.jobcenter.com/
http://www.ipa.com/
http://www.vjf.com/
http://www.emory.edu/CAREER/Links.html
http://usjob.net/
http://jobweb.com/catapault/emplyer.htm
http://www.gnatnet.net/~jgrothe/links.htm
http://www.headhunter.net/
http://www.americasemployers.com
http://www.nationjob.com/engineering
http://www.ajb.dni.us
http://www.jobweb.org/catapult/catapult.htm
http://www.austinknight.com/na/
http://www.mbajob.com/
http://www.dmworld.com/jobcenter/jobwant.html
http://www.jwtworks.com:80/tvjf/
http://www.lendman.com/
http://www.careerexpo.com/
http://www.jobweb.org/search/cfairs/
http://www.helpwanted.com
http://hitechcareer.com
http://www.careermart.com
http://www.golden.net/~archeus/worksrch.htm

If you are thinking of relocating, or are interested in job opportunities only in a particular region, you can do a regional search by signing on to one of the Web sites run by local business periodicals and the business sections of local newspapers nationwide. The sources are listed by state and come courtesy of the *"Local and Regional Business Publications on the Web"* section of *Harvard Business School's Baker Library* Web site: ***http://library.hbs.edu/localbiz***.

15

Intelligence Community Headhunters

The following headhunters specialize in recruiting individuals with backgrounds in intelligence and special operations. Since these recruiters are always looking for qualified candidates, you may want to let them know about your interests, skills, and experience.

Lee Thomas Careers
4832 Park Avenue
Bethesda, MD 20816
Tel: 301/320-0655
800/840-4094
E-mail: leethomas@aol.com

MTS Information Services, Inc.
CandidatePool
4938 Hampden Lane, Suite 337
Bethesda, MD 20814
301/229-9854
Fax: 301/229-9015
E-mail: mtswashdc@aol.com

The Wilshire Group
1595 Spring Hill Road
Suite 350
Vienna, VA 22182
703/847-5150
Fax: 703/847-3044

Wallach Associates, Inc.
6101 Executive Blvd., Suite 380
Box 6016
Rockville, MD 20849-6016
301/231-9000
Fax: 301/770-9015
E-mail: jobs@wallach.org

EPC Associates, Inc.
154 Leary Road
#268
Wagontown, PA 19376-0268
610/857-1800
Fax: 610/857-1805
E-mail: resumes@epcinc.com
http://www.epcinc.com

16

US Companies In Defense or Intelligence-Related Work

The following organizations do a great deal of intelligence-related work for various government agencies. Serving as contractors and consultants, they offer numerous job opportunities for individuals with intelligence and special operations backgrounds.

AAI Corporation
P.O. Box 524
Hunt Valley, MD 21030
Fax: 410/628-3191

ADI Technology Corporation
1029 N. Royal Street, Suite 200
Alexandria, VA 22314
Fax: 703/548-7882
http://www.aditech.com

Advanced Communications
Systems, Inc.
10089 Lee Highway
Fairfax, VA 22030-1734

AEGIS Research Corporation
7799 Leesburg Pike
Suite 1100N
Falls Church, VA 22043
703/847-6070

Aerotek, Inc.
7301 Parkway Drive
Hanover, MD 21076
800/927-8090
Fax: 410/712-7155

AlliedSignal Aerospace
111 South 34th Street
Phoenix, AZ 85034

Alphatech, Inc.
50 Mall Road
Burlington, MA 01803
Fax: 617/273-9345
E-mail: hr@alphatech.com

American Management Systems, Inc.
12601 Fair Lakes Circle
Fairfax, VA 22033
703/227-6470
Fax: 703/227-7266

American Systems Corporation
ASC HR Staffing
14200 Park Meadow Drive
Chantilly, VA 20151-2219
Fax: 703/968-5151
E-mail: recruiting@ascacc.com

Amsec International
P.O. Box 367
Middleburg, VA 20118
800/447-5070 or 540/687-6859
http://www.lidea.com/amsec/

Analysis & Technology
Human Resources Department
3241 Jefferson Davis Highway, Suite 1250
Arlington, VA 22202
703/418-2800
Fax: 703/418-8565
http://www.aati.com

Analytical Systems Engineering Corporation
5 Burlington Woods
Burlington, MA 01893

Andersen Consulting
Washington DC
1666 K Street, N.W.
Washington, DC 20006
202/862-8000
Fax: 202/785-4689
http://www.ac.com

Anser
1215 Jefferson Davis Highway
Suite 800
Arlington, VA 22202
Fax: 703/416-4451
E-mail: jobs@anser.org
http://www.anser.org

ARCA Systems
8229 Boone Blvd.
Vienna, VA 22180
703/734-5611
Fax: 703/790-0385

ARINC, Inc.
2551 Riva Road
Annapolis, MD 21401-7465
www.arinc.com

ARIST Corporation
P.O. Box 25517
Alexandria, VA 22313

ASW Group (S.O.C.)
Dept. WWW
170 NE 2nd Street
Suite 1043
Boca Raton, FL 33429-1043
Home Office—Deerfield Beach, FL
800/742-1560
E-mail: aswgroup@aol.com
http://home.navisoft.com/usintel

AT&T Federal Systems Advanced Technologies
1120 20th Street, NW, Room 501
Washington, DC 20036

Augmentation, Inc.
1738 Elton Road
Suite 100
Silver Spring, MD 20903
Fax: 703/431-3168

Autometric, Inc.
5301 Shawnee Road
Alexandria, VA 22312
703/658-4000
http://www.autometric.com

Aviation Technology Systems (ATS)
P.O. Box 3364
Manassas, VA 20108-0946
Fax: 703/330-0043
E-mail: atscorp@erols.com

Avtec Systems
10530 Rosehaven Street
Suite 300
Fairfax, VA 22030
Fax: 703/273-1313

Ball Aerospace & Technologies Corp.
P.O. Box 1235
Broomfield, CO 80038-1235
http://www.ball.com

Battelle
505 King Avenue
Columbus, OH 43201-2693
800/201-2011
National Security programs at Battelle: 888/201-2011

BBN Corporation
1300 North 17th Street, Suite 1200
Arlington, VA 22209
Fax: 703/284-2766
E-mail: kholmqui@bbn.com
http://www.bbn.com

BDM International Inc.
1501 BDM Way
McLean, VA 22102-3396
703/848-5000 or Fax: 703/848-6101
http://www.bdm.com

Bell Atlantic Professional Services
8180 Greensboro Drive, Suite 550
McLean, VA 22102
800/333-1213

Betac International
2001 N. Beauregard Street
Alexandria, VA 22311
703/824-3100
Fax: 703/824-0333

Boeing Defense & Space Group
P.O. Box 3999
M/S 80-PF
Seattle, WA 98124-2499
206/773-1230 or Fax: 206/773-3432

Booz, Allen & Hamilton, Inc.
8283 Greensboro Dr.
McLean, VA 22102-8283
703/902-5853
Fax: 703/902-3374
http://www.bah.com

BRI
P.O. Box 15505
Alexandria, VA 22309

Brightstar, Inc.
113 Center Drive North
North Brunswick, NJ 08902

BSG Alliance/IT, Inc.
8850 Stanford Blvd., Suite 4000
Columbia, MD 21045
Fax: 410/872-5450

BTG, Inc.
1945 Old Gallows Road
Vienna, VA 22182
http://www.btg.com/jobs/

CACI Inc. Federal
1100 North Glebe Road
Arlington, VA 22201-4798
703/698-4660 or Fax: 703/641-4914
http://www.caci.com

California Microwave, Inc.
6022 Variel Ave
Woodland Hills, CA 91367
818/922-8000
FAX: 818/712-5079

CAS, Inc.
Personnel Dept.
P.O. Box 11190
Huntsville, AL 35814
205/895-8949 or Fax: 205/895-8939
http://www.cas-inc.com

The CENTEC Group. Inc.
4200 Wilson Blvd., Suite 700
Arlington, VA 22203
Fax: 703/525-2349
E-mail: hrdept@centechgroup.com
www.centechgroup.com

Century Technologies, Inc.
8405 Colesville Road, Suite 400
Silver Spring, MD 20910
Fax: 301/588-1619
E-mail: resume@centech.com

CMB Technologies, Inc.
12310 Pinecrest Road, #105
Reston, VA 20191
Fax: 703/758-2621
E-mail: CMB1@aol.com
http://www.CMBTECH.com

The CNA Corporation
4401 Ford Avenue
Alexandria, VA 22302
Fax: 703/824-2740

Coleman Federal
490 L'Enfant Plaza, SW
Suite 7170
7th Floor
Washington, DC 20024
202/484-9393

Coleman Research Corporation
Human Resources, MS333
9891 Broken Land Parkway
Suite 200
Columbia, MD 21046
www.crc.com

Command Technologies, Inc.
405 Belle Air Lane
Warrenton, VA 22186
540/349-8623
Fax: 540/347-7105

Communications Systems Technology, Inc.
3800 Concorde Parkway, Suite 100
Chantilly, VA 20151
Fax: 703/968-7827

Computer Data Systems, Inc. (CDSI)
One Curie Court
Rockville, MD 20850
301/921-7000

Computer Professionals
P.O. Box 66075
Washington, DC 20035-6075
Fax: 202/887-8445

Computer Science Corporation (CSC)
3170 Fairview Park Drive
Falls Church, VA 22042
703/641-2140
http://www.csc.com

Computer Technology Services, Inc.
1700 Rockville Pike
Suite 315
Rockville, MD 20852
Fax: 301/231-7119

**Computers, Consulting, Systems
& Training, Inc. (CCS&T)**
7900 Sudley Road
Suite 800
Manassas, VA 20109
Fax: 703/368-7286

Computing Devices International
8800 Queen Ave., South
Bloomington, MN 55431
612/921-6120
Fax: 612/921-6490

Compex Corporation
5500 Cherokee Ave.
Suite 500
Alexandria, VA 22312
E-mail: resume@compexhq.com
http://www.compexhq.com

Condor Systems, Inc.
2133 Samaritan Drive
San Jose, CA 95124
408/371-9580 or Fax: 408/371-7589

Connectware
12120 Sunset Hills Rd., Suite 170
Reston, VA 22090-3231

Critical Intervention Services, Inc.
1265 S. Missouri Avenue
Clearwater, FL 34616
813/461-9417
Fax: 813/449-1269
E-mail: cis@webcom.com
http://www.webcom.com/cis/welcome.html

CTA Space Systems
1521 Westbranch Drive
McLean, VA 22102
Fax: 703/883-2657

D. Appleton Company
12500 Fair Lakes Circle, Suite 325
Fairfax, VA 22033
Fax: 703/631-5780
E-mail: staffing@dacom.com
http://www.dacom.com

Data Systems Analysts, Inc.
10400 Eaton Place, Suite 500
Fairfax, VA 22030
Fax: 591-8418
http://www.dsainc.com

DCS
1330 Braddock Place
Alexandria, VA 22314
Fax: 703/684-7229
http://www.dcscorp.com

David Sarnoff Research Center
CN 5300
Princeton, NJ 08543-5300
609/734-2000
Fax: 609/734-2040
E-mail: employment@sarnoff.com
http://www.sarnoff.com

Delfin Systems
Corporate HQ
3000 Patrick Henry Dr.
Santa Clara, CA 95054
408/748-1200
Fax: 408/748-1140

Digital Audio Company
5121 Holly Ridge Drive
Raleigh, NC 27612
Fax: 919/782-6766

Digital Equipment Corporation
6406 Ivy Lane
Greenbelt, MD 20770
301/918-5100
Fax: 301/918-5072
http://www.digital.com

DSTI
1700 Research Blvd.
2nd Floor
Rockville, MD 20850
Fax: 301/315-9688 or 301/610-0144
E-mail: staffing@dsti.com

Dynamic Systems, Inc.
635 Slaters Lane, #100
Alexandria, VA 22314
Fax: 703/684-4068

Dynamic Decisions, Inc.
1600 Wilson Blvd., Suite 1268
Arlington, VA 22209
Fax: 703/812-8888

Dynamics Research Corporation
1755 Jefferson Davis Highway
Suite 802
Arlington, VA 22202
703/412-2812 or Fax: 703/412-5086
http://www.drc.com

DynCorp
2000 Edmund Halley Drive
Reston, VA 22091-3436
703/264-0330

Eastman Kodak Company
1447 St. Paul Street
MC-37004
Rochester, NY 14653

Edgesource Corporation
2231 Crystal Drive
Suite 500
Arlington, VA 22202
Fax: 703/486-5708

EDS Military Systems Division
13600 EDS Drive
Herndon, VA 22071

EG&G Washington Analytical Services Center
1396 Piccard Drive
Rockville, MD 20850-4323
301/840-3000
Fax: 301/258-9522

E-Systems
Falls Church Division
7700 Arlington Blvd.
Falls Church, VA 22046
703/560-5000

Evans & Sutherland Computer Corporation
P.O. Box 58700
Salt Lake City, UT 84158

Executive Protection Associates, Inc.
Worldwide Headquarters
316 California Avenue
Reno, NV 89509
408/556-0430
E-mail: info@iapps.org

Executive Security International (ESI)
Gun Barrel Square
2128 Railroad Ave.
Department W
Rifle, CO 81650
800/874-0888
E-mail: duggan@esi-lifeforce.com/

FC Business Systems
Suite 700
5205 Leesburg Pike
Falls Church, VA 22041
Fax: 703/931-7804

Futron Corporation
7315 Wisconsin Ave.
Suite 900W
Bethesda, MD 20814
Fax: 301/907-7125
E-mail: resume@futron.com

GDE Systems, Inc.
P.O. Box 509008
San Diego, CA 92150-9008
619/592-1683
Fax: 619/592-1628

General Dynamics Corporation
1850 Centennial Park Dr.
Suite 400
Reston, VA 22091
703/264-0657
Fax: 703/264-7873

Geologics
5285 Shawnee Road
Suite 210
Alexandria, VA 22312
703/750-4000
Fax: 703/750-4010
http://www.geologics.com

Global Intelligence Applications
1708 King Mountain Road
Charlottesville, VA 22901

Government Systems Inc.
14200 Park Meadow Drive
Suite 200
Chantilly, VA 20151
Fax: 703/802-8376
E-mail: careers@gsimail.gsinet.com

Granite Island Group/TSCM.COM
127 Eastern Avenue #291
Gloucester, MA 01931-8008
978/546-3803

GRC International Inc.
1900 Gallows Road
Vienna, VA 22182
703/506-5000
Fax: 703/448-6890
E-mail: jobs@grci.com
http://www.grci.com/

Grumman Aerospace Corporation
South Oyster Bay Road
Bethpage, NY 11714
516/575-5186
Fax: 516/575-5836

GTE Government Systems Corporation
1001 19th Street, North, Suite 1100
Arlington, VA 22209

The Guild Corporation
8260 Greensboro Drive, Suite 460
McLean, VA 22102
703/761-4029
Fax: 703/761-4024
http://www.guildhome.com

Halifax Corporation
P.O. Box 888
Cascade, MD 21719
Fax: 301/241-3768

Harris Corporation, Electronic Systems Sector
P.O. Box 37
Melbourne, FL 32902

HCI Technologies, Inc.
11419 Sunset Hills Road
Suite 300
Reston, VA 20190
703/736-3019

Heckler & Koch Inc.
21480 Pacific Blvd.
Sterling, VA 20166-8903
703/450-1900
Fax: 703/450-8160

Helms International Group
8000 Towers Crescent Drive
Suite 1350
Vienna, VA 22182

High Technology Consultants
10530 Warwick Avenue
Suite C-4
Fairfax, VA 22030
703/218-2801
Fax: 703/218-2802
E-mail: htech@erols.com

Honeywell
7900 Westpark Drive
Suite A530
McLean, VA 22102-4299
703/734-7830
Fax: 703/734-7889

Horizons Technology, Inc.
700 Technology Park Drive
Billerica, MA 01821-4196

Houston Associates, Inc.
1010 Wayne Avenue
Suite 1200
Silver Spring, MD 20910
Fax: 410/495-8935

HR Advantage, Inc.
P.O. Box 10319
Burke, VA 22009
703/978-4029

Hughes Information Technology Corporation
1768 Business Center Drive
Reston, VA 22090

Ilex Systems
1838 Paseo San Luis
Sierra Vista, AZ 85635
520/458-9759
FAX: 520/458-3013

Image Graphics, Incorporated
917 Bridgeport Avenue
Shelton, CT 06484

Infodata Systems, Inc.
12150 Monument Drive
Fairfax, VA 22033
Fax: 703/934-7154
E-mail: hr@infodata.com

Information Spectrum, Inc.
1235 South Jefferson Davis Highway
Suite 507
Arlington, VA 22202
703/416-4000
Fax: 703/416-7726

Infosystems Technology, Inc.
6411 Ivy Lane
Suite 306
Greenbelt, MD 20770

Infotech Development, Inc.
3611 South Harbor Blvd.
Suite 260
Santa Ana, CA 92704

INNOLOG
2010 Corporate Ridge
McLean, VA 22102-7838
703/506-1555
Fax: 703/506-0827
E-mail: hrresume@hq.innologc.om

International Security, Inc.
1498 M Reisterstown Road
Suite 326
Baltimore, MD 21208
410/252-9787
Fax: 410-252-4319
http://www.intlsecurity.com/

IPA International
Personnel Manager
8133 Leesburg Pike, Suite 360
Vienna, VA 22182

ITT Defense & Electronics
1650 Tysons Blvd., Suite 1700
McLean, VA 22102
703/790-6300
Fax: 703/790-6360

Jane's Information Group
1340 Braddock Place, Suite 300
Alexandria, VA 22314
800/824-0768 or 703/683-3700
Fax: 800/836-0297 or 703/836-1593
E-mail: iwr@janes.com
http://www.awpi.com/intelweb/

Jaycor
9775 Towne Centre Drive
San Diego, CA 92121
http://www.jaycor.com

J.G. Van Dyke & Associates
5510 Cherokee Ave.
Suite 300
Alexandria, VA 22312
http://www.jgvandyke.com

The John Hopkins University
Applied Physics Laboratory
Johns Hopkins Road
Laurel, MD 20723
Fax: 410/792-5004

Keane Federal Systems, Inc.
1375 Piccard Drive
Suite 200
Rockville, MD 20850
301/548-4404
Fax: 301/548-1047

Litton Industries, Inc.
21240 Burbank Blvd.
Woodland Hills, CA 91367

Litton Systems, Inc.
Amecom Division
5115 Calvert Road
College Park, MD 20740

Lockheed Martin Corporation
6801 Rockledge Drive
Bethesda, MD 20817
301/897-6000
Fax: 301/897-6652

Lockheed Martin Management & Data Systems
10803 Parkridge Blvd., Suite 400A
Reston, VA 22091

Lockheed Martin Federal Systems
9500 Godwin Dr.
Manassas, VA 20110-4157
703/367-2121
http://www.lockheed.com

LOGICON
10400 Eaton Place
Fairfax, VA 22030
703/385-0190
Fax: 703/385-1987

Logicon Eagle Technology/
Logicon Information Technology Group
2100 Washington Boulevard
Arlington, VA 22204-5710
Fax: 703/920-7086

LORAL—Western Development Labs
3200 Zanker Road
San Jose, CA 95134

LORAL Federal Systems
9500 Godwin Dr.
Manassas, VA 22110
Fax: 703/367-3640

LORAL Defense Systems-East
9255 Wellington Road
Manassas, VA 22110
Fax: 703/367-4097

LSA Inc.
1215 Jefferson Davis Highway
Suite 1300
Arlington, VA 22202
lsa@pipeline.com

Magnavox Electronic Systems Company
1700 North Moore Street, Suite 1801
Arlington, VA 22209

ManTech Systems Engineering Corporation
1560 Wilson Blvd., Suite 1000
Arlington, VA 22209

Mantech International Corporation
14119-A Sullyfield Circle
Chantilly, VA 20151
Fax: 703/814-4201

Mead Data Central, Inc.
9443 Springboro Pike
Miamisburg, OH 45343

METRO Resources, Inc.
145 Lake Forest Drive
Fredricksburg, VA 22406
540/659-2734
Toll-free: 888/765-8222

MITRE Corporation
1820 Dolley Madison Blvd.
McLean, VA 22102-3481
Fax: 703/883-1369
E-mail: resume@mitre.org
http://www.mitre.org

Mitretek Systems
Corporate Recruitment
7525 Colshire Drive
McLean, VA 22102-7400
Fax: 703/610-1952
E-mail: staffing@mitretek.org
http://www.mitretek.org

Mnemonic Systems Incorporated
2001 L Street, NW, Suite 1000
Washington, DC 20036
Fax: 202/785-2531
E-mail: msihumre@erols.com

Motorola Government Electronic Group
P.O. Box 1417
Scottsdale, AZ 85252
http://www.mot.com/

MPRI
1201 East Abingdon Drive, Suite 425
Alexandria, VA 22314
703/684-0853
Fax: 703/684-3528

MRJ Inc.
10560 Arrowhead Drive
Fairfax, VA 22030
703/385-0700 or Fax: 703/385-4637

Mystech Associates, Inc.
5205 Leesburg Pike
Suite 1200
Falls Church, VA 22041
703/671-8680
Fax: 703/671-8932

NEI
1609 Maryland Avenue
Suite 539
Beltsville, MD 20704
Human Resources Dept.
Fax: 301/937-7476
E-mail: nei@ix.netcom.com

Nichols Research
1604 Spring Hill Road, Suite 200
Vienna, VA 22182-7510
Fax: 703/893-2572
http://www.nichols.com

Nichols Research Corporation
4040 South Memorial Parkway
Huntsville, AL 35802
205/883-1140
Fax: 205/880-0367

NOVA Security Services
9540 Courthouse Road, Suite 100
Vienna, VA 22181
703/281-7400
1/800/228-NOVA
Fax: 703/281-0888

Northrop Grumman Corporation
1840 Century Park East
Los Angeles, CA 90067
310/553-6262
Fax: 310/201-3023

OAO Corporation
Greenbelt, MD

Old Dominion Systems
P.O. Box 1834
Frederick, MD 21702-0834
301/662-8766
Fax: 301/662-9032

OMNIPLEX World Services Corporation
8000 Westpark Drive
Suite 200
McLean, VA 22102

Oracle Corporation
500 Oracle Parkway
Box 659425
Redwood Shores, CA 94065

ORION Scientific Systems
8400 Westpark Drive, Suite 200
McLean, VA 22102-3522
703/917-6540
Fax: 703/917-0394

ORION Research, Inc.
19800 Macarthur Blvd., Suite 480
Irvine, CA 92715
714/261-0226
Fax: 714/261-0243

Pacific-Sierra Research Corporation
1400 Key Blvd., Suite 700
Arlington, VA 22209
703/527-4975

Paul-Tittle Associates, Inc.
1485 Chain Bridge Road, Suite 304
McLean, VA 22101
Fax: 703/893-3871
E-mail: best100@Paul-Tittle.com

Performance Engineering Corporation
3949 Pender Drive
Fairfax, VA 22030
703/277-3308
Fax: 703/273-9881

Phoenix Consulting Group
Federal Services Practice
6725 Odyssey Drive
Huntsville, AL 35806
205/971-6741
E-mail: pcg-info@intellpros.com

Phoenix Systems, Inc.
1801 Alexander Bell Drive, Suite 650
Reston, VA 20191
703/264-2442
Fax: 703/264-2078
E-mail: phoenixPDS@aol.com

Pinkerton Computer Consultants, Inc.
1900 North Beauregard Street
Suite 200
Alexandria, VA 22311-1722
Fax: 888/820-7772
E-mail: resumes@pcci.com

PRB Associates, Inc.
43865 Airport View Drive
Hollywood, MD 20636
301/373-2360
http://www.prb-cam.com

PRC, Inc.
1500 Planning Research Center Drive
McLean, VA 22102
703/556-1000
Fax: 703/556-1174
E-mail: resumix@resumix.prc.com
http://www.careermosaic.com/cm/prc

Presearch Inc.
8500 Executive Park Ave.
Fairfax, VA 22031
703/876-6400
Fax: 703/876-6411

Profiles Threat Counter Measures
19672 Stevens Creek Boulevard
Suite 215
Cupertino, CA 95014
408/865-0951
Fax: 408/273-6082
E-mail: profiles@profiles-threat.com
http://www.profiles-threat.com/

Prosoft
2200 Clarendon Blvd.
Suite 1110
Arlington, VA 22201
Fax: 703/516-0474
E-mail: carwisee@ncr.disa.mil

PSC, Inc.
12330 Pinecrest Road
Reston, VA 22091
703/716-5000
Fax: 703/716-5005

PSYTEP Corporation
101 North Shoreline Blvd.
Suite 205
Corpus Christi, TX 78401
512/887-0079
Fax: 512/887-0955
E-ail: client_services@psytep.com

Quality Systems Incorporated
4000 Legato Road, Suite 1100
Fairfax, VA 22033
Fax: 703/352-9216

QuesTech, Inc.
7600-W Leesburg Pike
Falls Church, VA 22043
800/336-0354

RAND Corporation
1700 Main Street
P.O. Box 2138
Santa Monica, CA 90407-2138
Fax: 310/451-7024
http://www.rand.org

Rascal Communications, Inc.
5 Research Place
Rockville, MD 20850
301/208-7629
Fax: 301/208-7640

Raytheon Company
141 Spring Street
Lexington, MA 02173
617/862-6600
Fax: 617/860-2172

RDR, Inc.
P.O. Box 3279
Oakton, VA 22124
Fax: 703/273-8170
E-mail: resume@rdr.com

Research Planning, Inc.
Hurlburt Field Opportunities
6400 Arlington Blvd. #1100
Falls Church, VA 22042
Fax: 703/237-8085
E-mail: resume@rpihq.com

Rincon Research Corporation
101 N. Wilmot Road
Suite 310
Tucson, AZ 85711
520/519-4604
Fax: 520/519-4747

RMS Information Systems, Inc
4221 Forbes Blvd.
Lanham, MD 20706
Fax: 301/306-4474

Rockwell International
2201 Seal Beach Blvd.
Seal Beach, CA 90740
310/797-3311
Fax: 310/797-5828

Rosslyn Personnel, Inc.
Randolph Towers
4001 N. Nineth Street
Suite 226
Arlington, VA 22203
Fax: 703/243-7310

RPI
Corporate Headquarters
6400 Arlington Boulevard
Suite 1100
Falls Church, VA 22042
703/237-8061
E-mail: web-info@rpihq.com
http://www.rpihq.com

RS Information Systems, Inc. (RSIS)
1651 Old Meadow Road
5TH Floor
McLean, VA 22102
Fax: 703/902-0211

SAIC
1710 Goodridge Drive
McLean, VA 22102
http://www.saic.com

Science & Applied Technology, Inc.
Human Resources
21050 Califa Street
Woodland Hills, CA 91376
Fax: 818/887-2809

SDS International
2011 Crystal Drive
Suite 100
Arlington, VA 22202-3709

Security Concepts & Training, Inc.
Corporate
2533 N. Carson Street
Carson City, NV 89706
702/841-2739 or 800/839-2126
E-mail: corporate@sctinc.net
http://www.sctinc.net/general-information/mainpageindex.htm

SETA
6862 Elm Street
McLean, VA 22101
Fax: 703/821-5720
E-mail: resume@seta.com
http://www.seta.com

Signal Processing Systems
6855 Deerpath Road, Suite C
Baltimore, MD 21227

SIGTEK
9841 Broken Land Parkway
Suite 206
Columbia, MD 21046
410/290-3918
FAX: 410/290-8146
E-mail: info@sigtek.com
http://www.sigtek.com/sigtek

Silicon Graphics Computer Systems
12200-G Plum Orchard Drive
Silver Spring, MD 20904

SMCo
Standard Missile Company
1505 Farm Credit Drive
McLean, VA 22102

The Smith Corporation
13874 Park Center Road
Herndon, VA 20171-3216
Fax: 703-925-0329

Smith & Wesson
2100 Roosevelt Ave.
Springfield, MA 01102-2208
413/781-8300
Fax: 413/731-8980

SOZA International
Corporate Headquarters
8550 Arlington Blvd.
Fairfax, VA 22031
703/560-9477
Fax: 703/575-9026
http://www.soza-intl.com

Space Applications Corporation
901 Follin Lane, Suite 400
Vienna, VA 22180
703/242-4010
Fax: 703/255-5237

Sparta, Inc.
7926 Jones Branch Drive
Suite 900
McLean, VA 22102
E-mail: resume@mclean.sparta.com

Special Services Group
17762 Preston Road
Suite 100
Dallas, TX 75252
972/447-0077
Fax: 972/447-9929

SRA International Inc.
2000 15th Street North
Arlington, VA 22201
703/558-4700
Fax: 703/558-4723
http://www.sra.com

SRI International
333 Ravenswood Avenue
Menlo Park, CA 94025-3493
415/326-6200
Fax: 415/326-5512

SRS Technologies
1401 Wilson Blvd.
Suite 1200
Arlington, VA 22209
Fax:703/522-2891

SSI Services, Inc.
8500 Leesburg Pike
Vienna, VA 22182
Fax: 703/761-9512

Stanford Telecom
1761 Business Center Drive
Reston, VA 20190-5333
E-mail: acs-hr@sed.stel.com
http://www.stel.com

Stanley Associates, Inc.
300 N. Washington Street, Suite 400
Alexandria, VA 22314

Sterling Software, Inc.—ITD
1650 Tysons Blvd., Suite 800
McLean, VA 22102
703/506-0800
E-mail: resume_mclean@mclean.sterling.com

STG, Inc.
3702 Pender Drive
Suite 250
Fairfax, VA
Fax: 703/691-1810
E-mail: recruiting@stginc.com
http://www.stginc.com

STI
1383 General Aviation Drive
Melbourne International Airport
Melbourne, FL 32935
407/253-0209

Sun Microsystems Federal, Inc.
2650 Park Tower Drive
Vienna, VA 22180
http://www.sun.com

Sybase, Inc.
6550 Rock Spring Drive, Suite 800
Bethesda, MD 20817

SYNECTICS Corporation
10400 Eaton Place
Fairfax, VA 22030

System Planning Corporation (SPC)
1000 Wilson Blvd.
Arlington, VA 22209-2211
703/351-8200
Fax: 703/351-8567

System Technology Services, Inc.
8101 Sandy Spring Road
Suite 105
Laurel, MD 20707
Fax:301/498-1595

Systems Engineering Group, Inc.
9861 Broken Land Pkwy., Suite 350
Columbia, MD 21046-1170
Fax: 410/309-1942

Systems Planning and Analysis, Inc.
2000 N. Beauregard Street, Suite 400
Alexandria, VA 22311-1712
Fax: 703/931-9254
E-mail: resumes@spa.com
http://www.spa.com

TAD Resources International
1402 Shepard Drive
Sterling, VA 20164
800/853-1084
Fax: 703/450-6042

TASC
12100 Sunset Hills Road
Reston, VA 20190-3233
703/834-5000
http://www.tasc.com

TECH-ED Services
5430F Lynx Lane, #308U
Columbia, MD 21044
301/621-5105 or 410/740-0161
Fax: 410/740-9264

Techmatics
2231 Crystal Drive
Suite 1000
Arlington, VA 22202
Fax: 703/920-3928
E-mail: career@techmatics.com
http://www.techmatics.com

Technology Management Associates
10300 Eaton Place, #400
Fairfax, VA 22030
703/385-5400
Fax: 703/385-1786

Telos Consulting Services
2070 Chain Bridge Road, Suite 360
Vienna, VA 22182
703/506-1556
Fax: 703/506-1789
E-mail: telos.consulting@telos.com

Texas Instruments Defense Systems & Electronic Group
P.O. Box 660246
Dallas, TX 75266-0246
214/480-2447
Fax: 214/480-1677

The Orkand Corporation
7799 Leesburg Pike, Suite 700N
Falls Church, VA 22043-2499
Fax: 703/610-4230
E-mail resumes@orkand.com
http://www.orkand.com

Titan Systems, Inc.
1900 Campus Commons Dr.
Reston, VA
703/758-5600

Tracor Inc.
45 West Gude Drive
Rockville, MD 20850-1154
301/231-2199
Fax: 301/231-3290

TRW Space & Electronics Group
One Space Park Drive
Redondo Beach, CA 90278-1001
310/812-4693
Fax: 310/814-4507

TRW System Integration Group
One Federal Systems Park Drive
Fairfax, VA 22033-4411
ATTN: Recruiting Dept.
Fax: 703/803-5715
E-mail: resumes@iedweb.fp.trw.com

Unified Industries Incorporated
6551 Loisdale Court, Suite 400
Springfield, VA 22150
Fax: 703/971-5892

UNISYS Corporation
12010 Sunrise Valley Drive
Reston, VA 22091

US INTERNATIONAL
Corporate Intelligence Services

Vanguard Research, Inc.
10400 Eaton Place, Suite 450
Fairfax, VA 22030
Fax: 703/273-9398
www.vriffx.com

Vaxcom Services, Inc.
2106B Gallows Road
Vienna, VA 22182
Paul Warren, President
703/556-9058 or Fax: 703/556-7879
E-mail: rpwarren@vaxcom.com

Vector Data Systems
1100 South Washington Street, Suite 300
Alexandria, VA 22314
703/683-8327

Vector Research
3206 Tower Oaks Blvd., Suite 400
Rockville, MD 20852
Fax: 301/816-5517

Vitro Corporation
45 West Gude Drive
Rockville, MD 20850

Wang Federal, Inc.
7900 Westpark Drive
McLean, VA 22102-4299
703/827-3694
Fax: 703/827-6998

Watkins-Johnson Company
700 Quince Orchard Road
Gaithersburg, MD 20878
Fax: 301/921-9479 / 948-5527
E-mail: WJGB>JOB@WJ.COM
http://www.wj.com

WALCOFF
12015 Lee Jackson Highway, #500
Fairfax, VA 22033
FAX: 703/934-9866

Weiland Associates Group
3802 Great Neck Ct.
Alexandria, VA 22309

Welkin Associates, Ltd.
11300 Eaton Place
Suite 410
Fairfax, VA 22030

Wheat International Communications Corporation
8229 Boone Boulevard
Suite 360
Vienna, VA 22182

Wilbanks Technologies Corporation
2231 Crystal Drive
Suite 500
Arlington, VA 22202
Fax: 703/486-5709

WJB & Associates, Inc.
462 Herndon Parkway
Suite 205
Herndon, VA 20170
Fax: 703/742-9564

XonTech, Inc.
Corporate Human Resources
6862 Hayvenhurst Ave.
Van Nuys, CA 91406
Fax: 818/904-9440

Zachty-Parsons-Sundt, A Joint Venture
P.O. Box 14506
Harlandale Station
San Antonio, TX 98214-0506

17

The Corporate Directory

The following companies frequently or occasionally hire from the Military/Intel/SpecOp communities. The annotated listing is by no means exhaustive. Given today's rapidly changing business environment, some of these companies may move, change telephone and fax numbers, go out of business, and emphasize new operations. As a result, some of information may be dated by the time you use it. Since many of these companies have Web sites, you may want to use the various search engines to find current information on particular companies. When in doubt, call Information for the current telephone number or consult the latest annual edition of the *Business Phone Book USA* (Omnigraphics).

AAI Corporation
York Road
Cockeysville Hunt Valley, MD 21030
Fax: 410/628-3191

A defense, electronics, and manufacturing company, AAI was founded in 1950. With 1,100 employees is currently is one of Baltimore's leading employers, AAI had annual revenues in 1993 and 1994 of $216 million.

The company's primary source of revenue: [95%] is government sales, which according to the Baltimore Sun includes the National Security Agency, with only 5% from non-government customers. The primary business focus is 90% products and 10% services. Major corporate/institutional divisions are: Defense Systems, Weather Systems, Fluid Test Systems, Transportation Systems, and Firefighter Training Systems.

Adroit Systems, Inc.
209 Madison St.
Alexandria, VA 22314

Advanced Paradigms Inc. [API]
1725 Duke Street
Suite 200
Alexandria, VA 22314

API is a six-year old Virginia-based firm that provides applications development, communications and training solutions to Federal Agencies and commercial organizations nationwide. To meet the demand of a growing market, API has sustained an annual growth rate of over 130%. API's commercial client base includes organizations such as The Washington Post, National Public Radio, Sallie Mae, Freddie Mac, and Microsoft Corporation. API maintains strategic partnerships and subcontracts with such firms as CSC, DEC, Unisys, AT&T/NCR, WANG, EDS and Federal Data Corporation that span numerous Federal contracts and agencies. Federal clients includes such agencies as the Department of Veteran's Affairs, the Department of Transportation/FAA, the Department of State, the U.S. Postal Service, and the U.S. Senate. API also sells to the intelligence community, including the National Maritime Intelligence Center and the Drug Enforcement Administration.

Aegis Research Corporation
1735 North Lynn Street
Rosslyn, VA

Aegis Research was one of the corporate sponsors of the 1995 symposium at which the Corona program and product was declassified.

The Aerospace Corporation
Corporate Headquarters
El Segundo, CA 90245-4691
http://www.aero.org

Other Addresses:

Washington Corporate Office, 1000 Wilson Boulevard, Suite 2600, Arlington, VA 22209-3988

Herndon Office, The Hallmark Building, 13873 Park Center Road, Suite 187, Herndon, VA 22071

Columbia Office, 8840 Stanford Blvd., Columbia, MD 21045

Westfields Corporate Center, Chantilly, VA

Sunnyvale Office, Sunnyvale, CA 94088-0937

Western Range, Vandenberg AFB, CA 93437-0068

Eastern Range, Kennedy Space Center, FL 32815-0205

The Aerospace Corporation is a nonprofit corporation which operates a Federally Funded Research and Development Center serving as an architect-engineer for advanced space systems. It is the integral engineering arm for U.S. national security space and launch system programs. The corporate complex includes 16 owned or leased office buildings as well as research and technical facilities in El Segundo, California, three miles from Los Angeles International Airport. More than 3,100 people are employed by The Aerospace Corporation. Approximately 66 percent are members of the technical staff. The product of its efforts is government access to advanced space-based meteorological, early warning, intelligence, navigation, and communication capabilities, and associated launch vehicles and ground stations. The corporation's primary customer is the Space and Missile Systems Center (SMC) of Air Force Materiel Command, although work is performed for other agencies. The National Systems Group provides support to the National Reconnaissance Office. Aerospace is planning a building adjacent to the NRO offices in Westfields.

AlliedSignal, Inc.
Technical Services
One Bendix Road
Columbia, MD 21045
http://www.alliedsignal.com

Headquarters: Morristown, NJ

AlliedSignal Inc. is an advanced technology and manufacturing company headquartered in Morristown, NJ, and employs 83,500 people in three major business units: Engineered Materials Services; Automotive, and Aerospace, located in Torrance, CA, with 38,700 employees. The corporation had $11.8 billion in sales in 1993.

Alliant TechSystems
Signal Analysis Center
401 Defense Highway
Annapolis, MD 21401

Alliant provides products and services to the military, law enforcement and other information security customers. Areas of expertise include Tempest, high speed digital cryptography, and quick reaction capabilities for military and intelligence programs.

Amdahl Corp.
Worldwide Headquarters
1250 East Arques Avenue
Sunnyvale, CA 94088-3470
http://www.amdahl.com:80

Federal Service Corporation
12020 Sunrise Valley Dr., Suite 380
Reston, VA 22091

With over 1,600 major customer sites worldwide, Amdahl Corporation is a leader in developing and integrating large-scale systems and enterprise-wide solutions that address the business and information needs of leading organizations worldwide. The company is a value-added reseller of high performance computing systems to the national security community.

AmerInd Inc.
1310 Braddock Place
Alexandria, VA 22314

AmerInd provides information technology and services for commercial customers and the federal government, including the Unmanned Air Vehicle Joint Program Office.

AMP, Incorporated
Harrisburg, PA 17105
http://www.amp.com/welcome.html

AMP Aerospace and Government Systems Sector

Connectware Headquarters, Richardson, TX

Connectware [formerly VITec], 8605 Westwood Center Drive, Vienna, VA 22182

Connectware [formerly VITec], 12120 Sunset Hills Road, Suite #170, Reston, VA 22090

M/A-COM Inc. 100 Chelmsford St., Lowell, MA 01853

M/A-COM Inc. Government Products Division, 10713 Gilroy Rd, Hunt Valley, MD 21030

AMP is a leading developer and manufacturer of a wide variety of electronic and electrical interconnection devices. Founded in 1941, the company employs over 35,000 people in 38 countries and has 1994 sales exceeding $4 billion. AMP products can be found in almost any product that conducts electricity or uses electronics or optical signals: satellites, aircraft, automobiles, trucks, trains, ships, computers, telephone equipment, switching and outside plant equipment, consumer electronics and household appliances.

Connectware is an emerging leader in multimedia and advanced networking technologies. Connectware provides image manipulation and display software for users having specific interests in imagery, reconnaissance and intelligence applications (VITec ELT), as well as IDEX-class exploitation for interactive flicker free roam and pan of very large national images at full resolution (VITec VIPER). Connectware also provides a variety of high-performance, low-cost solutions for Sun SPARCstations that accelerate the display and manipulation of 24-bit true color images (RasterFlex Accelerators) and display real-time video (Raster Video). In addition the company's technology focus addresses not only traditional LANs, but also the convergence of LANs and WANs through ATM workstation interfaces and network switches (Cellerity products).

M/A-COM, with annual sales of $340 million, is a leading component supplier to the fast growing wireless communications market. Major product areas include a broad array of gallium arsenide and silicon-based semiconductor devices, coaxial cable connectors, and miniature antennas. The largest market served is cellular telephone. M/A-COM's Microelectronics Division's facilities are among the largest in the world for manufacture of gallium arsenide-based integrated circuit devices. The Government Products Division [the former Adams-Russell Micro-Tel Division] has sales of approximately $10 million in microwave surveillance signal receivers and calibration equipment and satellite and microwave communications equipment.

The Analysis Corporation
Arlington, VA

The Analysis Corporation supports CIA's Surveillance, Collection and Operations Support subgroup of the Technology Support Working Group, Office of Special Technology, 10530 Riverview Road, Fort Washington, MD 20744

Analytical & Research Technology Inc.
10565 Lee Hwy.
Suite 300
Fairfax, VA 22030

This privately held information systems development and integration services company, founded in 1988, has 35 employees with annual sales of over $5 million. On 1 December 1995 the Air Force Electronic Systems Center awarded a five-year $929 million contract for the Integration for Command, Control, Communications, Computers and Intelligence (IC4I) program to BTG and Cordant. This small-business set-aside procurement will supply the intelligence community with hardware, software and integration services focused on manufacture and development of interoperable systems and subsystems to upgrade the Intelligence Data Handling System and other systems. Cordant's team includes TRW Inc., Logicon Inc., Analytical Research Technology Inc. and GTE Services. BTG's principal teammates are EDS. and Sterling Software Inc.

Analytical Systems Engineering Corp
5 Burlington Woods
Burlington, MA 01893

This privately-held company, founded in 1969, has approximately 400 employees with annual sales of nearly $45 million in engineering and installation of building security systems.

Apcom Inc.
8-4 Metropolitan Court
Gaithersburg, MD 20878

Apcom provides digital signal processing and recording systems for COMINT, ELINT and signal collection, processing and analysis.

Applied Signal Technology Inc.
Headquarters
400 West California Ave
Sunnyvale, CA 94086
http://www.appsig.com

East Coast Engineering Office
10102 Avenel Garden Lane
Silver Spring, MD

Applied Signal Technology designs, develops, manufactures and markets signal processing equipment to collect and process a wide range of telecommunication signals. This equipment is used for signal reconnaissance of foreign telecommunications by the United States government and for a variety of applications in consumer products in the private sector. Signal reconnaissance systems are composed of collection equipment and processing equipment. Collection equipment consists of sophisticated receivers that scan the radio frequency spectrum (which includes, for example, cellular telephone, microwave, ship-to-shore, and military transmissions) to collect certain signals from among potentially thousands of signals. Processing equipment, using sophisticated software and hardware, evaluates the characteristics of the collected signals and selects signals that are likely to contain relevant information.

Purchases by intelligence agencies of the United States government have historically accounted for almost all of the Company's revenues, which are over $50 million annually. The Company devotes significant resources toward understanding the United States government's signal reconnaissance goals, capabilities and perceived future needs. The Company believes that it has much more marketing contact with customers and potential customers than is customary among its competitors. The Company's United States government customers consist of five defense and intelligence agencies with signal reconnaissance needs. Within these five agencies, the Company has contracts with approximately 20 different offices, each with separate budgets and contracting authority.

Gary L. Yancey, a co-founder of the Company, has served the Company as President and Chairman of the Board since the Company's incorporation in January 1984. Prior to co-founding the Company, he was employed for 10 years by ARGOSystems, a manufacturer of electronic reconnaissance systems. Several of the current officers of the company are also former employees of Boeing's ARGOSystems subsidiary.

The Company's business requires that it maintain at each of its offices a facility clearance sponsored and approved by the United States government. The Company leases four buildings (51,851, 52,464, 15,392 and 76,379 square feet) in Sunnyvale, which are used as the Company's headquarters and include development, engineering, production, marketing, and administrative offices. The Company leases a 15,250 square foot building in Herndon, Virginia which houses a small development facility and marketing and administrative offices. The Company leases a 6,300 square foot building in Jessup, Maryland which also houses a small development facility and marketing and administrative offices. The Company has also entered into new lease agreements for two new 58,000 square feet facilities to be constructed at the Company's headquarters in Sunnyvale, California, commencing July 1995 and December 1997.

Arca Systems Inc
2540 North First Street
Suite 301
San Jose, CA 95131

Arca Systems provides information systems security guidance, planning, and training for a variety of commercial and government customers, including the Maryland Procurement Office [NSA].

ARINC
Headquarters
2551 Riva Road
Annapolis, MD 21401
http://www.arinc.com

Other Addresses:

Vint Hill Farms Station, 6599 Commerce Court, Suite 203, Gainesville, VA 22065

Colorado Springs, 1925 Aerotech Drive, Suite 212, Colorado Springs, CO 80916

ARINC Incorporated is a $280 million company with a corporate heritage of serving customers in aviation, government, and other industries since 1929. ARINC employs more than 2,000 people at over 50 operating locations worldwide. ARINC provides communications services, systems development and integration, systems engineering, and management services to the world's aviation community, commercial customers, and government agencies such as the FAA, DoD, NASA, DOE, and DOT. ARINC provides sophisticated communications and information handling services capable of reaching aircraft anywhere in the world.

The Research Division is ARINC's largest, most wide-ranging business area. This division supports many types of advanced technology systems, including aircraft, satellite, navigation, communications, information, and industrial processes. The Research Division provides both government and commercial customers with systems engineering, software development, and complete systems integration solutions to complex operational requirements.

ARINC is the prime support contractor to US Army Space Command for the Army Space Based Exploitation Program (ASEDP), which demonstrates the effectiveness of space systems in supporting Army missions.

Arvin Industries, Inc.
One Noblitt Plaza
Columbus, IN 47202
http://www.arvin.com

Other Addresses:

> Space Industries International, Inc, 800 Connecticut Ave. Northwest, Suite 111 Washington, DC 20006

> Space Industries International, Inc, 101 Courageous Drive, League City, Texas 77573

> Systems Research Laboratories [SRL], Dayton, OH

Arvin Industries is a holding company with subsidiaries involved in diverse fields such as automotive parts and aerospace products and services. Arvin has over 13,000 employees and annual sales of over $2 billion.

Space Industries International [SII] is organized into four major divisions: Calspan Advanced Technology Center (Calspan ATC, Buffalo, NY), Systems Research Laboratories (SRL, Dayton, OH), Service Contracts Division (SCD, Tullahoma, TN), and Space Industries Division (SID, Houston, TX). Programs range in scope from multi-million-dollar contracts using interdepartmental support to small-scale research, design, development, engineering and operations of aerospace and space-support facilities, spacecraft and experiment equipment.

Calspan was originally formed in 1946 as the Cornell Aeronautical Laboratory, Inc., as part of Cornell University (located in Ithaca, New York). In 1972, the laboratory was reorganized as Calspan Corporation, a publicly-held company. In 1978, Calspan was acquired by Arvin Industries, and recently was merged with Texas-based Space Industries, Inc. to form SII.

With 600 employees and over $80 million in sales, SRL produces high resolution simulation and training monitors, automated inspection systems, and engineering services and support. On 29 January 1996 SRL was awarded a $14,500,000 indefinite delivery/indefinite quantity contract for scientific and technical analysis support for the National Air Intelligence Center, Wright-Patterson AFB, OH. The contract is expected to be completed January 2001.

ASIC International Inc.
2902 Tazewell Pike
Suite G
Knoxville, TN 37918
http://www.asicint.com

Other Addresses:

3060 Mitchellville Road
Suite 219
Bowie, MD 20716

ASIC International was founded in 1993. Its principals previously played key executive and technical roles with LSI Logic and Audio Animation, a developer of leading digital audio technology and equipment. AI's principals have been serving clients since 1965, and the company offers the industry's most experienced design experts to support Advanced Systems and complex application specific integrated circuit [ASIC] designs . AI serves customers worldwide. Their customer base includes industry leaders as well as early stage companies, and NSA's Maryland Procurement Office.

Astronautics Corp. of America
Headquarters
4115 N. Teutonia
Milwaukee, WI, 53209

Other Addresses:

Washington Office, 4717 Eisenhower Ave #-B, Alexandria, VA 22304

Kearfott Guidance and Navigation Corp., 150 Totowa Road, Wayne, NJ 07470

Little Falls, NJ

Asheville, NC

Brownsville, TX

Matamordos, Mexico

The Astronautics Corporation of America is an independent privately owned company founded in 1958. With annual sales of over $400 million and more than 3,000 employees, the company manufactures a wide variety of aerospace and defense electronics.

Kearfott Guidance and Navigation Corporation, formerly known as the Singer Company, was formed in 1917 and currently has over 2,200 employees who design and manufacture inertial guidance and navigation systems. The company also in engaged in system integration, precision components, testing, logistics and maintenance. Kearfott inertial reference units have been used on numerous civil, military and commercial science and communications satellites, such as AXAF, EOS, Galileo, Magellan, MILSTAR, TDRSS and DSCS, along with many sensitive military surveillance programs.

AT&T
Headquarters, Federal Systems, Advanced Technologies
1120 20th St. NW
Washington, DC 20036
http://www.att.com/findex.html
http://www.att.com/press/0393/930322.fsa.html
http://www.att.com/press/0194/940103.fsa.html

Other Addresses:

1919 South Eads Street, Suite 203, Arlington, VA 22202

Finksburg, Carroll County, MD

AT&T Paradyne

AT&T Secure Communications Systems

AT&T is the world's networking leader, providing commun-ications services and products, as well as network equipment and computer systems, to businesses, consumers, communications services providers and government agencies. AT&T was incorporated in 1885, but traces its lineage to Alexander Graham Bell and his invention of the telephone in 1876. AT&T's business units are the basic operating units of the company. Corporate organizations and divisions, such as finance, network services and human resources, provide cross-business unit support. The business units generally fall within four broad groups: Communications Services, Multimedia Products, AT&T Global Information Solutions, and Network Systems. Revenues grew in 1994 to a record $75.1 billion. The AT&T switched network is engineered for typical traffic of 175 million calls on an average business day.

AT&T Federal Systems is the largest defense contractor in North Carolina, with 2,600 employees in the Greensboro area. Additionally, Federal Systems has 1,000 employees in Whippany, N.J., 500 in the Washington, D.C., area, and 300 at other domestic and international locations. AT&T Advanced Technology Systems, Federal Systems Advanced Technologies's defense electronics business, is an independent business unit within AT&T Multimedia Products and Services. Its primary businesses are Integrated Underwater Surveillance Systems, Government Signal Processing and Digital Studio Systems.

AT&T Secure Communications Systems is part of AT&T Paradyne. AT&T Paradyne has annual sales of approximately $300 million in more than 90 countries and a work force of about 1,300. The secure communications group's major products are the Surity line of communications products, including products for secure voice, data, fax, video and cellular communications, and a variety of secure software programs. AT&T announced on 18 October 1995 that it is seeking offers from other companies for the purchase of AT&T Paradyne, based in Largo, FL.

Autometric, Inc.
5301 Shawnee Rd.
Alexandria, VA 22312
NMIA Sponsor
http://www.autometric.com

1330 Inverness Drive
Colorado Springs, CO 80910

From its founding in 1957 as a subsidiary of Paramount Pictures, Autometric has become the market leader providing information systems and services in reconnaissance and remote sensor imagery-related areas. Autometric compiles the latest in processing and display hardware with state-of-the-art data management software for space operations to theater combat, from interactive terrain visualization to a geographically-enhanced transportation system.

Autometric has been involved in national security electro-optical, synthetic aperture radar, and multispectral imagery reconnaissance programs for over 30 years. Specific products which receive, manage, and manipulate imagery data in support of military operations include DataMaster for staging national imagery for image exploitation, and the Naval Tactical Command System-Afloat Image Exploitation Work-stations (NIEWS). Russian Imagery Services from a variety of optical sensors with 2-10 meters resolution and from a radar sensor with 15-30 meters resolution offers coverage over areas previously unavailable at this image quality.

Ball Corporation
Headquarters
345 South High Street
Muncie, IN 47305
http://www.ball.com

Other Addresses:

Aerospace & Technologies Corp., Broomfield, CO

Ball Corporation produces metal beverage containers, metal food and specialty containers, international metal containers, and PET plastic containers. Aerospace & Technologies Corporation pro-vides products and services to government and commercial customers.

Ball Corporation entered the aerospace industry in 1956 with the acquisition of Control Cells Inc., a small research and development operation in Boulder, Colorado. Renamed Ball Brothers Research Corporation, its initial mission was to develop and use its technical expertise to improve Ball's glass manufacturing operations. Effective 6 August, 1995 the Ball Aerospace and Communications Group was renamed the Ball Aerospace & Technologies Corp.

Ball Aerospace & Technologies Corp. is a leading space systems and components and communications equipment manufacturer and integrator with $268 million in 1994 sales. Ball has two aerospace divisions: the aerospace systems division and the telecommunication products division. The aerospace systems division is comprised of four business units: electro-optical subsystems; sensors, cryogenics, pointing & tracking;

space systems; and systems engineering. The telecommunication products division is comprised of two business units: advanced antennas and video systems and communication and video products.

Ball has developed world-class capabilities in electro-optical instruments, space-based sensors, instrument pointing, object tracking, space-based cryogenics systems, and small- and medium-sized low earth orbit satellites. Ball also designs and produces commercial and military antenna and video products and provides systems engineering services and support. Ball's core expertise is in development and supply of equipment and services to convert observable phenomena into usable electronic data in the DoD, Intelligence, NASA, and Civil Space markets.

Locations include Pasadena, Sacramento and San Diego, CA; Boulder, Broomfield, Colorado Springs, Mead and Westminster, CO; Eglin Air Force Base, Florida; Warner Robins, GA; Wahiawa, HI; Lanham, MD; Albuquerque, NM; Dayton, OH; and Arlington and Dahlgren, VA.

BBN - Bolt, Beranek & Newman Corporation
Headquarters
150 Cambridge Park Drive
Cambridge, MA 02140
http://www.bbn.com/home.html

Other Addresses:

BBN Systems & Technologies
1700 North 17th Street
Arlington, VA

BBN's technical expertise and problem solving experience includes internetworking, data analysis, and collaborative systems and acoustic technologies with annual revenue of approximately $200 million. The company employs 2,000 professionals in offices around the world. From the ARPANET to the Internet, BBN has designed, built and maintained some of the largest networks for some of the world's most demanding government and commercial customers. BBN provides a range of network services, systems, and products, for use primarily by the US government under various contracts. BBN provides research, development, hardware, software, and professional services for wide-area networks supporting distributed simulation and training, warfighting simulation, and command and control functionality; advanced Internet routers supporting integrated video, voice, and data requirements; and cryptographic systems and products for sophisticated network security applications. Advanced networking technologies and related inter- and intra-networking applications include advanced speech recognition and language understanding capabilities, such as text spotting and gisting, that enable voice identification for network security applications, and the extraction of useful information from multiple electronic sources, including the Internet.

Betac Corporation
Headquarters
2001 N. Beauregard St.
Alexandria, VA 22312
703/824-3100
http://www.betac.com

Other Addresses:

> San Antonio Operations, Suite 510, 7323 Hwy. 90 West, San Antonio, TX 78227

> Colorado Springs Operations, Suite 205, 5050 Edison, Colorado Springs, CO 80915

> Fort Huachuca Operations, P.O. Box 2392, Sierra Vista, AZ 85636

Betac, a privately-held company founded in 1977 with over 200 employees, has annual sales of over $20 million in defense and government related services. Betac Corporation has locations all around the world, and many of Betac's sites within the United States are located near major military installations.

On 14 December, 1995 Betac was awarded one of two contracts with a combined $120 million ceiling by the US Air Force Space Warfare Center, Colorado Springs, CO, under the Tactical Exploitation of National Capabilities (TENCAP) program. Betac's initial tasks under the Space Warfare Center Operations Support Contract (SWCOSC) will be to provide education and training support and systems planning support to enhance combat operations by integrating national and Department of Defense space systems into command and control warfare (C2W), intelligence, and warfighting capabilities.

Additional tasks covered under the contract include support to the

SWC in the areas of requirements analysis, contingency support, and modeling and simulation to support Special Access programs. The Betac team, includes Aerojet, BDM, CSC Darlington, FRI, Hughes, I-NET, SAIC, TOE, and UNISYS.

Boeing
Headquarters
7755 East Marginal Way South
Seattle, WA 98108
http://www.boeing.com

Other Addresses:

Defense and Space Group, Seattle, WA
Missiles and Space Division, Huntsville, AL
Space Systems, Seattle, WA
Space Systems, Cape Canaveral AFS, FL
Space Systems, Sunnyvale, CA
Space Systems, Vandenberg AFB, CA
ARGOSytems, 430 N. Mary Avenue, Sunnyvale, CA 94086
324 N. Mary Avenue, Sunnyvale, CA 94086
884 Hermosa Court, Sunnyvale, CA 94086
Gilroy, CA
Redwood City, CA
7483 Candlewood Road, Hanover, MD 21076
Norfolk, VA

Information Services Group

Information Services, 7990 Boeing CT, Vienna, VA
Information Services TMIS, Suite 500, 1801 Alexander Bell Dr., Reston, VA

The Boeing Company, headquartered in Seattle, WA is the world's leading manufacturer of commercial airplanes. Boeing is organized into three major business segments: Commercial Airplane Group, Defense & Space Group, and Information & Support Services. In 1994, company revenues exceeded $21 billion—about 80 percent from commercial customers; 20 percent derived from US Government contracts. Boeing employs about 110,000 people in over 10,000 job categories. The company is a major US Government contractor, with capabilities in space systems, helicopters, military airplanes, missile systems, electronic systems and information systems management.

Defense and Space operations—conducted principally through Boeing Defense & Space Group—involve research, development, production, modification and support of military aircraft and helicopters and related systems, space systems and missile systems. Defense and Space sales are principally to the US Government, including classified projects. Defense and space segment revenues were $4.7 billion for 1994, compared with $4.4 billion and $5.4 billion for 1993 and 1992, respectively. The Company's defense and space business is broadly diversified, and no program accounted for more than 20% of total 1992-1994 defense and space revenues. US Government classified projects also continued to contribute to defense and space segment revenues.

Boeing expanded its information and aerospace capabilities with the purchase of the ARGOSystems defense electronics firm in 1987. ARGOSystems, with locations in Maryland, Virginia, and Texas, specializes in military electronics, research and development, and electronic systems hardware, including the AN/WLR-1H shipboard ESM system, which is capable of generating up to 128 simultaneous emitters over a frequency range of 0.5 to 18.0 GHz.

Other business activities include developing large-scale information systems and conducting management services through Boeing Computer Services, principally for government agencies. An information systems contract to enhance the readiness of the Army Reserve and National Guard units is currently the largest contributor to other business revenues, which declined to $331 million in 1994, down from $463 million and $622 million in the previous two years.

Booz, Allen & Hamilton, Inc.
Corporate Headquarters
Allen Building
8283 Greensboro Drive
McLean, VA 22102
703/902-5853
Fax: 703/902-3374
http://www.bah.com:80

Other Addresses:

14800 Conference Center Drive, Suite 300, Chantilly, VA 22021

Airport Square VIII, 891 Elk Ridge Landing, Linthicum, MD 21090

385 Moffett Park Drive, Suite 110, Sunnyvale, California 94089

Booz, Allen & Hamilton is an international management and technology consulting firm, founded in 1914, committed to helping senior management solve complex problems. One of the world's largest consulting firms, Booz, Allen has more than 75 offices around the globe. Clients include most of the largest industrial and service corporations in the world and departments and agencies of the US federal government, including US Departments of Defense, Justice, and Treasury; US, National Security and Intelligence Communities, with work including the Central Imagery Office's National Imagery Transmission Format Standards (NITFS). This private corporation, wholly owned by officers, has a staff of 6,000,worldwide.

Bourns, Inc.
1200 Columbia Ave.
Riverside, CA 92507

Other Addresses:

RECON-OPTICAL, Inc., 550 West Northwest Hwy., Barrington, IL 60010

RECON-OPTICAL, Inc./CAI Division, 550 West Northwest Hwy., Barrington, IL 60010

RECON-OPTICAL, Inc./Pacific Optical Division, 2660 Columbia St., Torrance, CA 90503

Bourns Incorporated is a privately-held company founded in 1947, with over 4,500 employees and annual electronics and photonics sales in excess of $250 million. The RECON-OPTICAL subsidiary of Bourns designs and manufactures aerial surveillance cameras with over 200 employees and annual sales of over $25 million. The CAI subsidiary has comparable, employment and sales, specializing in high resolution, high-speed long-range tactical reconnaissance cameras. The Pacific Optical operation, with about a quarter the employment and sales of the other two locations, specializes in optical components including lenses, prisms, mirrors and coatings.

Brightstar, Inc.
113 Center Drive North
North Brunswick, NJ 08902

BTG, Inc.
Headquarters
1945 Old Gallows Road
Vienna, VA 22182
http://www.btg.com

Other Addresses:

> BTG Technology Systems, 1768 Old Meadow Road, Westpark, McLean, VA 22103

> 839 Elkridge Landing Road, Linthicum Heights, MD 21090

> Annapolis Junction, MD

BTG provides systems development, integration and engineering services to the US Government [primarily the military], specializing in open systems development, systems engineering, reusable software, document management, value-added reselling, and the manufacture of customized high-performance computers. The company has 650 employees, including over 300 employees with Secret/Top Secret clearances. BTG's FY 1995 revenue of $156.0 million was 51% higher than the Constant Source Operator's Terminal (CSOT) that BTG developed for the US Air Force is an analysis workstation that correlates, displays and disseminates intelligence information. Story Teller is another BTG system that correlates data from signals intelligence for US Navy reconnaissance analysts, allowing them to exchange tactical information with other US forces. The Joint Deployable Intelligence Support System (JDISS), based primarily on commercial off-the-shelf [COTS] hardware and software, is a rapidly deployable system connecting communications and intelligence centers worldwide, across strategic, theater and tactical lines. Another program using BTG's integration expertise is the U.S. Special Operations Intelligence Vehicle (SOF-IV), a self-contained intelligence vehicle designed for worldwide use by US Special Forces. Under BTG's contract with the Air Force Information Warfare Center (AFIWC), the company performs system prototyping, software development and training, hardware procurement, and inspection and exercise support.

On 1 December, 1995 the Air Force Electronic Systems Center awarded a five-year $929 million contract for the Integration for Command, Control, Communications, Computers and Intelligence (IC4I) program to BTG and Cordant. This small-business set-aside procurement will supply the intelligence community with hardware, software and integration services focused on manufacture and development of interoperable systems and subsystems to upgrade the Intelligence Data Handling System and other systems. Cordant's team includes TRW Inc., Logicon Inc., Analytical & Research Technology Inc. and GTE Services. BTG's principal teammates are EDS. Intermetrics, and Sterling Software Inc.

Cadence
Corporate Headquarters
San Jose River Oaks Campus
555 River Oaks Parkway
San Jose, CA 95134

Other Addresses:

Maryland Sales Office
6760 Alexander Bell Dr.
#140
Columbia, MD 21046

Cadence Design Systems, Inc. is the leading supplier of business solutions for the design of electronic components and systems. It provides customers a combination of leading-edge software tools and professional design services to help optimize their product development processes. With 1995 revenues of $548 million, the company owns approximately 30% of the Electronic Design Automation (EDA) market and saw revenues increase by 28% over the past year. Cadence has more than 2,700 employees located throughout North America, Europe, Japan and the Pacific Rim. Formed in 1988 through the merger of two EDA industry pioneering companies, Cadence has established a reputation of technology leadership for the tools used in complex silicon and systems design.

California Microwave, Inc.
Corporate Headquarters
985 Almanor Ave.
Sunnyvale, California 94086
http://www.cmi-ged.com

Other Addresses:

> Government Electronics Division, 6022 Variel Avenue, Woodlands
> Hills, CA 91367

> Airborne Systems Integration Division, 1362 Brass Mill Road,
> Belcamp, Maryland 21017

California Microwave is one of the world's leading suppliers of products,
systems and turnkey telecommunications networks that capitalize on
microwave radio technology. Founded in 1968, California Microwave
has manufacturing operations in eight states and representatives
worldwide.

Government Electronics Division develops and integrates data
communication systems and capabilities for tactical military users. The
division integrates ground and airborne electronic systems for military
customers and is a provider of Tactical Data Link (TADIL), Mission
Information Management Systems (MIMS), and Systems Integra-
tion/Software Development Services. California Microwave is a major
provider of multi-sensor airborne reconnaissance systems which support
Air/Land/Maritime surveillance and intelligence activities. Airborne
Systems Integration (ASI) develops and integrates multi-sensor imaging
systems and advanced signals collection systems for airborne applications.

Camber
Headquarters
635 Discovery Drive
Huntsville, AL 35806

Other Addresses:

> 1755 Jefferson Davis Highway, Arlington, VA
> 5203 Leesburg Pike, Falls Church, VA
> 7411 Alban Station Court, Springfield, VA

Camber Corporation provides customized computer programming services.

Cambridge Research Associates
1430 Springhill Road
Suite 200
McLean, VA 22102

The company's PowerScene renders real-time, perspective views using actual terrain imagery (e.g. SPOT, LANDSAT, ADRI, CIB) and digital terrain elevation models (e.g. DTED, DEM), with dynamic and static models of man-made objects and cultural features. These functions along with leading-edge capabilities for data fusion have many applications including: military intelligence, analysis, mission preview, planning, rehearsal, and training. This application has received extensive publicity due to its use in Bosnia.

Cambridge Research Associates, a privately-held corporation with 40 employees, is owned in part by a joint holding called HQTP Strategic Investments Inc., a California-based limited partnership founded in 1986 by Defense Secretary William Perry [who is listed as the general partner], Undersecretary of Defense for Acquisitions Paul Kaminski, and Director of Central Intelligence John Deutch."Under an arrangement with the Senate Armed Services Committee, they are the first top officials in Defense Department history to maintain direct investments in military contractors while overseeing military contracts. The committee action created a double standard at the Pentagon. Senior military officers who oversee defense contracts are routinely forced to divest stock or other investments related to the defense industry." [Newsday 10 May 1995]

Carlyle Group
1001 Pennsylvania Avenue N.W.
Suite 220 South
Washington, DC 20004

Other Addresses:

BDM Headquarters, 1501 BDM Way, McLean, VA 22102

BDM Federal

1901 N. Moore Street, Arlington, VA 22209
4401 Ford Avenue, Alexandria, VA 22302
6432 General Green Way, Shirley Edsall Industrial Park, Alexandria,
   VA 22151
Skyline Towers I, 5205 Leesburg Pike, Falls Church, VA 22041
Skyline Towers IV, 5205 Leesburg Pike, Falls Church, VA 22041
9055 Guilford Road, Suite C, Columbia, MD 21046
9705 Patuxent Woods Drive, Columbia, MD 21046
3012 Merder Drive, San Antonio, TX 78325
Vinnell Corporation 12150 East Monument Drive, Suite 800, Fairfax,
   VA 22033
Sunnyvale, CA
Laredo, TX
San Antonio, TX
Pirinclik, Turkey

Chaired by former Defense Secretary and Deputy Director of Central Intelligence Frank Carlucci, the Carlyle Group, a merchant bank buyout fund, sold GDE Systems, a defense technology manufacturer, for about $100 million in November 1994. It acquired MagneTek Inc.'s power technology systems business for $35 million in November 1994. Acquired Power Paragon Inc. The Group agreed to sell Magnavox Electronic Systems Co., a defense-electronics maker for $370 million in September 1995.

BDM International, Inc. is a publicly held multinational information technology company that operates in three interrelated markets: Systems and Software Integration, Computer and Technical Services, and Enterprise Management and Operations through its four principal subsidiaries. Established in 1960 as Braddock, Dunn and McDonald, Inc. the company became BDM International in 1979, and was acquired by Ford Aerospace in 1988, BDM revenue has grown at a compound annual rate of 38% during the four years (1991-1994) since a management led buyout in 1990 from Ford Motor Company, by investors led by The Carlyle Group, L.P., including senior BDM management. The record 1994 revenue total of $774.2 million represented a 39% increase over the $558.3 million posted in 1993. Established in 1960, BDM has 7,000 employees at over 60 offices and locations worldwide. BDM Federal, Inc. is the largest subsidiary in the BDM family, employing over 3,200 people, including the National Security and Defense Group, which is helping create enterprise-wide IT strategies, standards, and solutions for agencies moving from mainframe-based computer systems to modern client/server environments.

Vinnell Corporation operates internationally in widely varying geographic locations and cultures, providing a broad spectrum of professional and technical services to government clients in multiple areas of management and operations (M&O) and military training. The Vinnell Corporation subsidiary of BDM also has been active in Saudi Arabia for many years. Vinnell teams perform a wide range of tasks encompassing logistics, training, planning, and maintenance support for the Saudi Arabian National Guard and other Saudi clients.

CAS Inc.
Corporate Headquarters
650 Discovery Drive
Post Office Box 11190
Huntsville, AL 35806
http://www.cas-inc.com

Other Addresses:

Washington Office, 1725 Jefferson Davis Highway, Arlington, VA

CAS, Inc. is a major DoD weapon system analysis contractor providing material development, combat development, test and evaluation, and operational user customers with complete engineering, analytical and automation services solutions. CAS provides system engineering and analysis support for theater missile defense, air defense, aviation, and land combat missile systems, and related surveillance, battle management, command, control, communications and computer systems.

Ceridian Corporation
8100 34th Ave. South
Bloomington, MN 55425

Other Addresses:

Computing Devices International, 8800 Queen Ave., South Bloomington, MN 55431

Computing Devices International, 141 National Business Parkway, Annapolis Junction, MD 20701

Paragon Imaging, 400 West Cummings Park, Suite 2000, Woburn, MA 01801

Sales Office, Crystal Gateway 2, Suite 800, 1225 Jefferson Davis Highway, Arlington, VA 22202

The former Control Data Corporation, Ceridian has over 7,500 employees generating annual sales of over $900 million.

Computing Devices International [formerly Control Data Corporation's Government Systems Group] has over 2,500 employees with annual sales of over $400 million of airborne and spaceborne computer systems. Computing Devices specializes system development and integration for SIGINT and IMINT processing and near real time information fusion and exploitation applications.

Paragon Imaging, a 35-employee division of Ceridian, was acquired by the company in 1988. Paragon Imaging products include the Electronic Light Table [ELT] Series is a product line of easy-to-use, affordable commercial off-the-shelf (COTS) imagery display and manipulation software tuned to the needs of DoD and civilian agencies. Approximately 70% of U.S. imagery analysts use Paragon's ELT software. The ELT Series is NITF certified under the JDISS, Sentinel Byte, ADNET, and IAS (Marines) programs.

Chrysler [Electrospace]
Chrysler World Headquarters
1000 Chrysler Drive
Auburn Hills, Michigan 48326

Other Addresses:

Chrysler Technologies Corporation,
Electrospace Systems, Inc, Richardson, TX 75083
Chrysler Technologies Airborne Systems

Chrysler Corporation was incorporated under the laws of the State of Delaware on March 4, 1986, and is the surviving corporation following mergers with a number of its operating subsidiaries, including Chrysler Motors Corporation which was originally incorporated in 1925. Chrysler Corporation and its consolidated subsidiaries operate in two principal industry segments: automotive operations and financial services. Chrysler also engages in aircraft modification and the manufacture of electronics products and systems through its Chrysler Technologies Corporation subsidiary.

Electrospace Systems, a Chrysler subsidiary, is a systems engineering company which applies integrated information systems to commercial, military and other government requirements. These include satellite earth stations, operations centers, and battlefield intelligence and electronic warfare systems. Founded in 1970, it was acquired by Chrysler Corporation in 1987. With Top Secret Clearances at all facilities, the company's more than 500,000 square feet of facilities include 300,000 Sq. Ft. of manufacturing and 200,000 Sq. Ft. of engineering & office space for nearly 1,200 employees.

On 26 October, 1995 Electrospace was awarded a $10,561,936 modification contract for the production of 14 TROJAN Special Purpose Integrated Remote Intelligence Terminal (SPIRIT) II Systems with no-cost warranty, and data. The TROJAN SPIRIT II system is an integration of commercial and non-developmental items (NDI) consisting of a High Mobility Multipurpose Wheeled Vehicle (HMMWV) mounted shelter with Mobile Antenna Platform (MAP) providing an intelligence processing and dissemination capability via Satellite Communications (SATCOM) in support of split-based operations; and, another HMMWV mounted shelter providing a Spare Equipment and Maintenance (SEM) capability. Work will be performed in Richardson, Texas, and is expected to be completed by December 30, 1998. The contracting activity is the U.S. Army Communications and Electronics Command, Warrenton, VA.

Command & Control Consulting Inc
406 North Pitt Street
Alexandria, VA 22314

C3I provides business and strategic development services and government relations support to a variety of information, technology clients, including DEC, Hughes, Loral, and Unisys.

Command Technologies Inc
405 Belle Air Lane
Warrenton, VA 22186

Other Addresses:

Engineering and Training Services (METS) Division, 6852 Alamo

Downs Parkway, San Antonio, TX 78238

Electronic Technology Application Division (ETAD), 1290 South Hwy. A1A, Satellite Beach, FL 32937

Command Technologies, Inc. (CTI) is a professional services firm providing system engineering, technical services, logistic support services, and training services to federal government clients, principally the Department of Defense. CTI's contracts and experience focus on software development, development of automated data processing capabilities, computer based training, and logistics support analysis and planning. CTI has grown from a one person company in 1988 to over 125 full time personnel. The Warrenton, San Antonio, and Satellite Beach facilities are cleared as Top Secret facilities with Secret storage by the Defense Investigative Service (DIS). The majority of CTI personnel possess high level security clearances; 60% are cleared at the SECRET or higher level up to and including TOP SECRET/ Sensitive Compartmented Information.

Functional areas encompassed within the scope of work include operational intelligence, intelligence support planning, threat analysis, theater missile defense (TMD), communications intelligence (COMINT), SENIOR FIX and other signals intelligence (SIGINT) and measurement and signature intelligence (MASINT). Clients include the Air Intelligence Agency (AIA), Air Force Information Warfare Center (AFIWC), Central MASINT Technology Coordination Office (CMTCO), Ballistic Missile Defense Office (BMDO), and the Air Force Technical Applications Center (AFTAC).

Computational Logic, Inc. [CLI]
1717 W. 6th St.
Suite 290
Austin, TX 78703-4776
http://www.cli.com/index-description.html

Computational Logic, Inc. (CLInc) is a small, employee-owned, computing research service company founded in 1983. CLI performs advanced research and development in mathematical modeling of digital hardware and software systems. CLInc provides services in applying mathematical modeling of hardware and software systems to AT&T, Boeing, Burroughs, DEC, Ford Aerospace, GTE, Honeywell, MCC, Motorola, Rockwell International, TRW, the US Government and others.

Computer Sciences Corporation
Corporate Office
2100 East Grand Avenue
El Segundo, CA 90245

Other Addresses:

Systems Engineering Division, 6565 Arlington Blvd., Falls Church, VA 22042

1100 West Street, Laurel, MD 20707

CSC solves client problems in information technology, with broad-based services including management consulting in the strategic use of information technology, systems integration, and outsourcing. CSC has a staff of 33,000 employees in 575 offices in major cities throughout the world and annual revenues of $3.4 billion, up 31% from the $2.6 billion reported the previous year.

CSC work includes software engineering support and technical information systems security applications services to the Department of Defense. CSC Geographic Information Systems (GIS) intelligence applications include processing remotely-sensed images to assess agricultural stability worldwide by modeling soils, vegetation, temperature and precipitation over areas of interest. The CSC Hughes Support Center business unit of over 1,000 IT professionals provides $200 million annual IT outsourcing services to Hughes Missile System Company.

Condor Systems
2133 Samaritan Drive
San Jose, CA 95124

Condor Systems is a privately-held company founded in 1981 with over 200 employees and annual sales of over $40 million. The company designs and builds antenna systems, receivers and automated signal collection and analysis systems for national intelligence agencies and DoD.

Cordant Inc.
11400 Commerce Park Drive
Reston, VA

On 1 December 1995 the Air Force Electronic Systems Center awarded a five-year $929 million contract for the Integration for Command, Control, Communications, Computers and Intelligence (IC4I) program to BTG and Cordant. This small-business set-aside procurement will supply the intelligence community with hardware, software and integration services focused on manufacture and development of interoperable systems and subsystems to upgrade the Intelligence Data Handling System and other systems. Cordant's team includes TRW Inc., Logicon Inc., Analytical Research Technology Inc. and GTE Services. BTG's principal teammates are EDS. and Sterling Software Inc.

CTA Incorporated
Headquarters
6116 Executive Boulevard
Rockville, MD 20852
http://www.cta.com

Other Addresses:

CTA Space Systems, 1521 West Branch Drive, McLean VA 22102

Founded in 1979, CTA has grown rapidly and today comprises over 1600 staff members nationwide with revenues in 1993 of $140 million. CTA specializes in applying multi-disciplinary teams of senior, experienced engineers, and scientists to client's needs involving complex aerospace systems.

Data General
Headquarters
4400 Computer Drive
Westboro, MA 01580
http://www.dg.com

Other Addresses:

7927 Jones Branch Drive #200, McLean, VA 22101

1190 Winterson Road, Linthicum Heights, MD 21090

Data General is an open systems company that specializes in providing servers, storage products and services to information systems users worldwide. With fiscal 1994 revenues of $1.12 Billion, the company employs approximately 5,800 personnel worldwide. More than 90 percent of Data General's product revenues come from open systems, primarily the AViiON family of servers which run DG/UX, the company's commercial UNIX operating system.

Data General's operating system, DG/UX, provides a robust file system, open connectivity, comprehensive systems and storage management, standards compliance, and applications scalability. In addition, with the recent introduction of the DSO Defense Security Option, DG/UX became the first multi-processor UNIX operating system to support B2 level security, complying with strict security standards set by US Government agencies.

Delfin Systems
Corporate Headquarters
3000 Patrick Henry Drive
Santa Clara, CA 95054
http://www.delfinsd.delfin.com/delfinsd

Other Addresses:

1450 Frazee Rd. Suite 708, San Diego, CA 92108

12007 Sunrise Valley Drive, Suite 300, Reston, VA 22091

1555 King Street, Alexandria, VA 22314

Delfin Systems provides analysis, development, and integrated systems solutions to signal exploitation, intelligence, and information resource management requirements for the defense and intelligence communities. Delfin expertise covers hardware and software engineering, artificial intelligence, signal processing, and operations analysis for collection and exploitation of signal intelligence, threat response processes, fusion and exploitation of all source intelligence, and analysis and assessment of intelligence data. Delfin Systems had total sales of $24 million 1994.

Delfin Systems is owned in part by the HQTP partnership of Defense Secretary William Perry, Under Secretary of Defense for Acquisition and

Technology Paul Kaminski, and Director of Central Intelligence John Deutch [which is also part-owner of Cambridge Research Associates].

Digital Equipment Corporation
Headquarters
111 Powdermill Road
Maynard, MA 01754
http://www.digital.com

Other Addresses:

> Digital Federal Government Region, 6406 Ivy Lane, Greenbelt, MD 20770

Digital Equipment, founded in August 1957, is a leading worldwide supplier of networked computer systems, software and services, with 61,700 employees and annual sales of over $13 billion. Digital pioneered and leads the industry in interactive, distributed and multivendor computing. An international company, Digital does more than half its business outside the United States, developing and manufacturing products and providing customer services in the Americas, Europe, Asia, and the Pacific Rim.

Based in Greenbelt, Maryland, Digital Federal Government Region is focused on providing solutions that enhance the operations and productivity needs of government customers. Digital has a comprehensive portfolio of industry-leading hardware, software, system, and network products, as well as systems and network integration, consulting, and multi-vendor services in the industry.

DEC's 64-bit Alpha render sophisticated models and simulations that were once the exclusive domain of super computers. Geographic Information Systems (GIS) mapping applications, and remote sensing, including high-resolution satellite images.

Digital Equipment Corporation along with Oracle Corporation and PRC Corporation demonstrated an innovative solution by which US and Allied Nations can share classified information and a common picture of the battle space. 13 servers, workstations, and personal computers along with software were integrated into JWID'95 the Joint Warrior Interoperability Demonstration. The Multilevel Releasability Server mounted on DEC's DISA-developed Ops/Intel Workstation Alpha-based computers includes a high security operating system from Digital called MLS+ and a high security SQL database from Oracle called Trusted Oracle7.

Docu-Data Corporation
Glen Burnie, MD

Docu-Data Corporation was awarded on October 1, 1995, a $1,048,000 increment as part of a $15,132,000 time and materials contract for engineering and technical documentation services performed at Fort Meade, Maryland.

Eastman Kodak Company
Headquarters
1447 St. Paul Street
Rochester, NY 14653
http://www.kodak.com
http://www.kodak.com/gov/aerialSystems/aerialSystems_home.sht ml

Other Addresses:

1300 North 17th Street, Suite 1040, Arlington, VA 22209

KODAK's Commercial and Government Systems provides imaging solutions to federal, state and local agencies and their prime contractors. Positioned as a supplier, system and sub-system integrator, C&GS technologies include acquisition, processing, analysis, transmission, management and storage of images.

There are five groups within KODAK's Commercial and Government Systems business unit. Imaging Products and Systems (IPS) specializes in design and integration of photographic and digital imaging systems for defense and intelligence agencies. IPS also provides field management, training and engineering services. Image Acquisition Systems (IAS) specializes primarily in ground-based, airborne, and spaceborne E-O image acquisition subsystems and systems for surveillance and remote sensing. IAS use special skills in the design and fabrication of optical systems and image sensor modules. KODAK is a major subcontractor to TRW for NASA's AXAF program.

Aerial Systems, the world's leading supplier of high-resolution aerial films and processing systems, serves a broad range of federal agencies including NASA, NOAA, USGS and USDA, as well as strategic and tactical military reconnaissance users. Aerial Systems also markets KODAK's digital imaging products to the remote sensing community.

Since the mid-1970s, Kodak has led the way in the development of solid-state image capture devices. In 1986, Kodak scientists designed and fabricated the world's first megapixel sensor—a sensor capable of recording 1.4 megapixels, or 1.4 million picture elements.

The company is a strategic partner with Space Imaging, which is planning to provide a commercial source of high-resolution satellite imagery. Other products include the Megapixel Imaging Technology (MITE), a high resolution COTS digital imaging capture system for Unmanned Aerial Vehicles (UAV) markets.

EDS
EDS Headquarters
5400 Legacy Drive
Plano, TX 75024-3199
http://www.eds.com/home.html

Other Addresses:

EDS Government Services Group

EDS Military Systems Division, 13600 EDS Drive, Herndon, VA 22071

1600 N. Beuaregard St., Alexandria, VA

5113 Leesburg Pike, Falls Church, VA

9636 Austin Way, Manassas VA,

Founded in 1962, Electronic Data Systems Corporation [EDS] became an independent subsidiary of General Motors in 1984. And on 7 August, 1995 General Motors announced that it intended by the first half of 1996 to pursue a split-off of EDS to its GM Class E shareholders in a tax-free exchange of stock through which EDS would become an independent, public company. GM shares tied to results of Electronic Data Systems trade under the symbol GME. EDS has approximately 80,000 employees worldwide and serves more than 8,000 customers. In 1994, EDS posted revenues of $10.05 billion. Sales and operations are the responsibility of 47 strategic business units, each oriented to a particular industry or geographic region.

The Company's business involves operations in principally one industry segment: designing, installing, and operating business information and communications systems. Revenues from GM contributed approximately 36%, 39%, and 41% of gross revenues for the years ended December 31, 1994, 1993, and 1992, respectively. On 1 December 1995 the Air Force Electronic Systems Center awarded a five-year $929 million contract for the Integration for Command, Control, Communications, Computers and Intelligence (IC4I) program to BTG and Cordant. This small-business set-aside procurement will supply the intelligence community with hardware, software and integration services focused on manufacture and development of interoperable systems and subsystems to upgrade the Intelligence Data Handling System and other systems. BTG's principal teammates are EDS, Intermetrics and Sterling Software Inc.

EG&G

Corporate Headquarters
EG&G Washington Analytical Services Center
1396 Piccard Drive
Rockville, MD 20850

Other Addresses:

2341 Jefferson Davis Highway, Arlington, VA 22202

8809 Sudley Road, Manassas, VA 22110

Remote Sensing Laboratory, Las Vegas, NV

EG&G, Inc., was formed in 1947 by three individuals whose initials the company now bears: Dr. Harold E. Edgerton, Mr. Kenneth J. Germeshausen and Mr. Herbert E. Grier. Dr. Edgerton was the inventor of the photographic strobe.

The Washington Analytical Services Center provides software engineering, prototype design and development and scientific analysis to a variety of customers, including military and intelligence agencies, their contractors and other commercial enterprises.

The Remote Sensing Laboratory supports CIA's Surveillance, Collection and Operations Support subgroup of the Technology Support Working Group, Office of Special Technology, 10530 Riverview Road, Fort Washington, MD 20744

EOSAT
4300 Forbes Boulevard
Lanham, MD 20706
http://www.eosat.com

EOSAT was formed in 1984 by Hughes and Lockheed Martin to commercialize the U.S. Landsat remote sensing satellite program. Since that time EOSAT has evolved into the market leader in the remote sensing industry offering products from a multitude of international satellite platforms. EOSAT currently markets an assortment of multi-spectral, panchromatic, and radar data in a range of spectral and spatial resolutions to a range of commercial and governmental customers, including the Defense Mapping Agency.

Energy Research and Generation
900 Stanford Avenue
Oakland, CA 94608

This privately owned independent company, with 25 employees and annual sales of $3 million, produces specialized open-celled metal foams made of aluminum, carbon, and silicon carbide. The use of low-density foams as core materials enables the design of strong, high-stiffness lightweight structures. National security applications have included nuclear weapons, strategic missiles, and reconnaissance satellites.

ETI
112 Elden Street
Suite Q
Herndon, VA 22070

ETI develops and markets digital data collection and signal processing systems.

Electronic Warfare Associates
13873 Park Center Road
Herndon, VA 22701

Electronic Warfare Associates provides hardware and software design and development, system engineering and digital signal processing.

FGM Inc.
131 Elden Street
Suite 308
Herndon, VA 22070
http://www.fgm.com/FGM_home.html

Other Addresses:

Honolulu, HI
San Diego, CA

FGM Inc. was founded in 1987 by Mike Fortier, Scott Gessay, and Mike Morehouse. FGM Inc. is a privately held corporation governed by a board of directors, with 38 employees located at 3 sites (as of May 31, 1995). FGM specializes in the development of command and control systems and supporting tools. Since its initial release in 1989, Macintosh Commanders Integrated Decision Support System [MacCIDSS] has evolved into a state-of-the-art map creation system with support for most Defense Mapping Agency (DMA) mapping products. In the current release of MacCIDSS, the background layer can be based on either CIA World Database II vector maps, Vector Product Format raster maps, or Defense Mapping Agency ARC Digitized Raster Graphics raster maps.

Forecast International / DMS
Headquarters
22 Commerce Road
Newtown, CT 06470
http://www.forecast1.inter.net

Forecast International produces a wide range of open-source intelligence products on defense and aerospace topics.

GenCorp, Inc
Headquarters
175 Ghent Road
Fairlawn, OH 44333

Other Addresses:

Aerojet Corporation, Highway 50 & Aerojet Road, Rancho Cordova, CA 95670

Azusa, CA
Colorado Springs, CO
Huntsville, AL
Los Angeles, CA
Socorro, NM
Washington, DC

GenCorp Inc. was incorporated in Ohio in 1915 as The General Tire & Rubber Company. The Company's operations are grouped into three business segments: its automotive business, its polymer products business and its aerospace and defense business, Aerojet-General Corporation. The Company currently employs approximately 13,000 persons.

Aerojet develops, manufactures and markets solid and liquid rocket propulsion systems, smart munitions systems, sensor surveillance systems, earth sensing systems and related defense products and services. Aerojet has concentrated for the past several years on obtaining contracts that provide a balance between technology development and long-term production, as well as between defense and space programs. More recently, efforts have been expanded to include the pursuit of non-defense domestic and international market opportunities that take advantage of the segment's technologies, engineering and manufacturing expertise and capabilities.

The aerospace and defense business' programs have included the Titan, Minuteman, Standard Missile, Advanced Solid Rocket Motor ("ASRM") and Delta propulsion programs; satellite surveillance sensor systems; the Sense and Destroy Armor (SADARM) program; earth sensing systems; TOW 2B armaments; Combined Effects Munition systems; ground data processing systems; and medium caliber ammunition programs.

Sales in 1994 for Aerojet were $594 million, down 32 percent from 1993 sales of $872 million. The decrease is due to the residual impact of the Peacekeeper program cancellation and the Advanced Solid Rocket Motor program termination, lower activity in the Sense and Destroy Armor and Tube-Fired Optically Tracked Wire programs and the sale of the Ordnance medium caliber ammunition and air dispensed munition businesses. Aerojet's direct and indirect sales to the United States Government and its agencies (principally the Department of Defense) were approximately $578 million in 1994, $846 million in 1993 and $982 million in 1992.

Determining the future role of Aerojet in the corporation is a key part of the Company's strategy. The Company is continuing to discuss the possibility of divestiture with interested parties while at the same time evaluating alternatives such as joint ventures, strategic alliances or continued operation of Aerojet should efforts to divest not offer adequate shareholder value.

The sale of all or part of Aerojet would reduce the Company's exposure to recent wide variability in defense spending and would allow the Company to focus on its growing commercial businesses. Any divestiture would initially reduce sales and segment operating profit until the Company is able to redeploy assets to businesses generating equal or better returns. The Company is required to use the proceeds from any sale of all or part of Aerojet to reduce outstanding debt under the Company's credit facility. Further, this credit facility would be reduced permanently by the amount of the net cash proceeds from any sale. The reduction in debt and interest expense would improve the Company's financial condition.

General Motors
General Motors Corporation
3044 West Grand Boulevard
Detroit, MI 48202

Other Addresses:

Hughes Electronics Corp Los Angeles, CA 90080
http://www.hughes.com

Hughes Research Laboratories, 3011 Malibu Canyon Road, Malibu, CA 90265
http://www.hrl.com

Hughes Aircraft Company, Los Angeles, CA

Radar and Communications Systems, El Segundo, CA 90009

Hughes Electro-Optical Systems, El Segundo, CA 90009

Hughes Danbury Optical Systems, 100 Wooster Heights Rd, Danbury, CT 07801

ITEK Optical Systems, 10 Maguire Road, Lexington, MA 02173

ITEK Optical Systems, Burlington, MA

ITEK Optical Systems, Sunnyvale, CA

Hughes Information Technology Corporation, 1768 Business Center Drive, Reston, VA 22090

SPONSOR

Hughes Information Technology Corporation, 1577 Spring Hill Road, Vienna, VA 22103

Hughes Training Link Division, 5111 Leesburg Pike, Suite 300, Falls Church, VA 22041

Hughes Telecommunications and Space Company

Hughes Space and Communications, El Segundo, California

Magnavox Electronic Systems Company Fort Wayne, IN

Magnavox Electronic Systems, 1700 N. Moore St., Arlington, VA 22209

General Motors is the world's largest manufacturer of cars and trucks, with total revenues of nearly $155 billion and 700,000 employees in 1994. The major portion of General Motors Corporation's operations are derived from the automotive products industry segment. GM also has financing and insurance operations and produces products and provides services in other industry segments. The other products segment consists of military vehicles, radar and weapon control systems, guided missile systems, and defense and commercial satellites; the design, installation, and operation of business information and telecommunication systems; as well as the design, development, and manufacture of locomotives.

GM Hughes Electronics manufactures defense electronic, weapons systems and automotive electronics, and operates a direct broadcast satellite television system. General Motors acquired Hughes Aircraft Company on 20 December 1985, and renamed this operation GM Hughes Electronics Corporation, which includes 33 major plants, offices, and research facilities. Since 1961, Hughes Space and Communications

Company, with its predecessors, the Space and Communications Group and the Hughes Space Systems Division, has engaged in the development and production of state-of-the-art space and communications systems for military, commercial, and scientific uses. Hughes Space and Communications integrated satellite factory in El Segundo, California, builds satellites. Hughes Training, Link Division (HTI/Link) is dedicated to the enhancement of human productivity in the workplace through the application of human factors and training technology. With the acquisition of Link from CAE Inc of Toronto, Link is a division of Hughes Training, the training subsidiary of GM Hughes Electronics.

On 11 September, 1995 Hughes Electronics announced that its Hughes Aircraft Co., subsidiary had agreed to purchase Magnavox Electronic Systems Co. for $370,000,000 in cash from the Carlyle Group. Magnavox Electronic Systems Company designs, develops, and manufactures commercial and military electronic systems and equipment. The Magnavox Electronic Systems Company's historical roots go as deep as 1911, the year it was founded in Napa, California as the Commercial Wireless and Development Company, which was recapitalized in 1917 as The Magnavox Company. The company was acquired in 1974 by the North American Philips Corporation, a US subsidiary of N.V. Philips, Eindhoven, Netherlands, from which it was purchased in October of 1993 by MESC Holdings, Inc., a company organized by the Carlyle Group. Magnavox provides a wide range of defense and commercial satellite communications products. Magnavox is a dominant supplier to DoD of signals intelligence electronic combat situational awareness and combat identification systems, such as the Integrated Data Fusion System.

On 15 November, 1995 Hughes Electronics announced plans to acquire the ITEK Division. Approximately 75% of ITEK's 270 employees will be moved to Hughes Danbury Optical Systems division, and the ITEK Lexington facility with be closed. Litton's ITEK ["Information Technology"] Optical Systems Division performs contract research and development for government customers, and is a leading supplier of imaging and image-processing equipment. With annual sales of over $50 million, 750 employees are housed in 270,000 square feet of facilities in Massachusetts, with support for fielded systems conducted from the Sunnyvale location.

Geodynamics Corp
21171 Western Ave
Suite 110
Torrance, CA 90501

Other Addresses:

Colorado Springs, CO

Geodynamics provides remote sensing and Geographic Information Systems support to commercial and military clients.

GRC International, Inc.
Headquarters
1900 Gallows Road
Vienna, VA 22182
http://www.grci.com

Other Addresses:

Crystal City, VA
Chantilly, VA
Columbia, MD
Colorado Springs, CO

Founded in Santa Barbara in 1961, GRC International, Inc. has been a leader in information technology, studies and analysis, modeling and simulation, and testing and evaluation. With 1,400 employees, more than 90% of GRC's $137 million revenues in 1995 resulted from supporting a wide spectrum of clients in the DoD, space and intelligence and civil communities with decision-support and productivity-enhancement products and services.

GTE
Headquarters
One Stamford Forum
Stamford, CT 06904

Other Addresses:

GTE Government Systems Corporation [GSC], 77 A Street, Needham Heights, MA 02194

GTE Government Systems Corporation [GSC], 1001 19th St. North, Arlington, VA 22209

GTE GSC Space Systems, 15000 Conference Center Drive, Washington Technology Park, Chantilly, VA 22021

GTE GSC Baltimore Technical Office, 3106 Timanus Lane, Suite 200, Baltimore, MD 21244

GTE GSC Baltimore Field Office, Airport Square Building AS-19, 1099 Winterson Road, Suite 110, Linthicum, MD 21090

GTE GSC Systems Integration and Support, 9821 Broken Land Parkway, Columbia, MD 21046

GTE GSC Space Systems Services Organization, 7404 Executive Park, Suite 501, Seabrook, MD 20706

GTE GSC Electronic Defense Systems Division [EDSD], 100 Ferguson Drive, Mountain View, CA 94043

GTE GSC EDSD Electronic Defense Intelligence and Collection Systems [EDICS], 100 Ferguson Drive, Mountain View, CA 94043

GTE GSC EDSD Intelligence, Communications & Processing Systems [ICPS], 1700 Research Blvd., Rockville, MD 20850

GTE GSC EDSD Intelligence, Information & Imagery Processing Systems [I3S], 1700 Research Blvd., Rockville, MD 20850

GTE GSC EDSD I3S Westlake Operations, 31717 La Tienea Drive, Westlake Village, CA 91362

GTE GSC EDSD I3S Colorado Springs Field Office,, 1050 South Academy Blvd., Colorado Springs, CO 80910

GTE GSC EDSD I3S Rome Field Office, Beeches Technical Campus, Route 26N Building 3, Rome, NY 13440

GTE GSC Information Systems Division

Chantilly Virginia Operations [Federal Systems Division] Washington Technology Park, 15000 Conference Center Drive, Chantilly, VA 22021-3808

GTE GSC Secure Communication Systems Division

GTE GSC SCSD 9821 Broken Land Parkway, Columbia, MD 21046

GTE Corporation has two major business segments: telephone operations and telecommunications products and services. In March 1991, the merger of GTE and Contel Corporation was consummated. GTE and its subsidiaries had approximately 117,000 employees, at 31 December 1993. GTE's telephone operating subsidiaries in the United States served approximately 17.1 million access lines in 33 states as of 31 December 1993 and provided many types of communications services, ranging from local telephone service for the home and office to highly complex voice and data services for various industries.

Telecommunications Products and Services consists of Personal Communications Services, which is comprised of GTE Mobilnet, Contel Cellular Inc. (CCI) and GTE Airfone, GTE Information Services, and GTE Government Systems.

In January 1994, GTE combined GTE Spacenet Corporation with GTE Government Systems Corporation. GTE Government Systems' primary business is the development, manufacturing and integration of customized command, control, communications and intelligence systems for the defense and national security agencies of the US Government. Spacenet provides a broad range of telecommunications services and systems for businesses, news organizations, educational institutions and government agencies throughout the US and in over 30 other countries. As of December 1993 the company operated eight communications satellites for the US domestic market.

GTE Government Sector Corporation employs over 4,500 people with facilities in a dozen states. Chantilly Operations includes Defense Information Systems, Civilian Information Systems, Space Systems, and the Telecommunications Service Organization. One of this location's largest customers is the Federal Aviation Administration.

GTE GSC's Electronic Defense Systems Division has over four decades of experience in all aspects of signals intelligence, intelligence processing, information warfare and imagery resource management. The division employs about 1,400 people, including 800 scientists and engineers, with some 250 personnel providing support at field operations. Electronic Defense Intelligence and Collection Systems work includes fixed and relocatable signals intelligence collection and processing systems. Intelligence, Communications & Processing Systems responsibilities include intelligence community communications systems, and signals intelligence collection, processing and distribution systems.

Intelligence, Information & Imagery Processing Systems is responsible for intelligence analysis, processing and data handling systems for DoD and the intelligence community, including imagery exploitation, processing, secondary dissemination, and storage.

DIA's National Military Intelligence Center / Collection Coordination Facility (NMIC/CCF) was in need of maintenance and upgrading in order to continue supporting the National Military Intelligence Center's mission requirements. GTE has maintained and enhanced the automated message handling system and other software applications of the NSS and CCFSS. GTE has also maintained and enhanced all related hardware, has procured and installed new hardware, and has developed and implemented numerous new and enhanced message handling capabilities. Major subsystem functions include: Advanced Imagery Requirements and Exploitation System (AIRES) Query.

GTE Information Systems Division provides telecommunications, networking, health care, aviation and weather services to the Department of Defense and other Federal agencies. GTE's Chantilly, Virginia facility operates the third largest node on the Internet. Space Systems provides telecommunications systems and services to support operational elements for U.S. Space Command. ISD furnishes systems engineering, communications systems, systems and information integration, databases, software, message processing and dissemination, display and data fusion to support the U.S. Air Force satellite network and related space programs.

Harris Corporation
Headquarters
1025 West NASA Boulevard
Melbourne, FL 32919
http://www.harris.com

Other Addresses:

Electronic Systems Sector, P.O. Box 37, Melborne, FL 32902

Government Aerospace Systems Division, P.O. Box 94000, Melbourne, FL 32902

Government Communication Systems Division, P.O. Box 91000 Melbourne, FL 32902

Information Systems Division, P.O. Box 98000, Melbourne, FL 32902

Harris Space Systems Corporation, Rockledge, FL

Harris Data Services Corporation, 1201 East Abingdon Drive, Alexandria, VA

Harris Telecommunications Systems Division, Building 1822, 6021 Abbot Road, Ft. Belvoir, VA, 22060

Harris Corporation is a worldwide company focused on four major businesses—electronic systems, semiconductors, communications, and office equipment—employing more than 30,000 people. Worldwide sales exceed $3 billion.

Electronic Systems Sector products include space systems such as processors, data busses, antennas, communication subsystems, and microwave sensing instruments. Communications systems include satellite TT&C (telemetry, tracking, and command), mobile/survivable/ transportable C3I (command, control, communication, and intelligence) systems, and tactical intelligence systems.

Information systems include real-time processing systems for: information processing, communications processing, signal processing, image processing, and command & control; algorithmic-intensive systems for signal processing, weather processing, image processing, natural language processing and neural network applications; analyst support systems built for: ELINT workstations, Imagery, weather analysis, SIGINT, and SIGINT expert workstations, including secure workstations and network management expert systems; data distribution, analysis, storage systems for intelligence data storage, message switching, and signal data analysis and distribution.

Harris Semiconductor, based in Melbourne, Florida, was founded in 1962 as the Microelectronics Division of Radiation, Inc. It became the Semiconductor Sector of Harris Corporation in 1967. The Sector's military and aerospace products include encryption and secure communications systems and components. The Harris Military and Aerospace Programs Operation includes responsibility for secure communications (COMSEC), tactical, strategic and space programs.

Horizons Technology, Inc.
700 Technology Park Drive
Billerica, MA 01821

With $17 million in annual revenue, Horizons Technology provides computer software for military aviation mission planning, and electro-optical models for aerial targeting.

HTR
Headquarters
6110 Executive Blvd.
Suite 810
Rockville, MD 20852

Other Addresses:

McLean, Virginia

Founded in 1987, HTR is an established, privately held corporation positioned as a full service client/server knowledge transfer company. Over the past eight years, HTR has grown from a small network integration company to an internationally recognized, full-service technology deployment organization, with growth rates exceeding 60% annually. Some of HTR's government clients include the Bureau of Alcohol, Tobacco, and Firearms and the Central Intelligence Agency.

IBM
Corporate Headquarters
One Old Orchard Road
Armonk, NY 10504
http://www.ibm.com

Other Addresses:

IBM Government Systems

Lotus Government Sales and Marketing, 1000 Wilson Boulevard, Arlington, VA 22209

Lotus Development Corp., Cambridge, MA

IBM Federal Systems Company, 6705 Rockledge Drive, Bethesda, MD 20718

IBM is in the business of providing customer solutions through the use of advanced information technologies. The company operates primarily in the single industry segment that creates value by offering a variety of solutions that include, either singularly or in some combination, services, software, systems, products, financing, and technologies. Total revenues in 1994 were $64 billion, compared to $62 billion in 1993.

On 11 June 1995 IBM and Lotus Development Corp. announced a definitive merger agreement under which IBM paid $64 per Lotus share in cash for all of Lotus' outstanding shares and preferred share purchase rights. The transaction had a total equity value of approximately $3.5 billion. Lotus Notes, the leading client/server platform for developing and deploying groupware applications, is IBM's workgroup client, and the Notes server product family is IBM's mail, messaging and groupware server platform. Lotus Notes supports all major shipping operating systems, including IBM OS/2 Warp, Microsoft Windows 3.1, Windows NT, Apple Macintosh (client only) and four UNIX platforms: IBM AIX, Sun Solaris, Hewlett-Packard's HP-UX and Santa Cruz Operation's OpenServer.

Lotus Development Corp. has released a Notes DMS [Defense Message System] version of its Notes groupware replacing commercial encryption with the Capstone encryption algorithm, the Digital Signature Standard (DSS) and the Message Security Protocol application programming interface developed by the National Security Agency. According to a 13 November 1995 article in Network World, "The Central Intelligence Agency, which uses Notes extensively, intends to migrate to Notes DMS in the future since federal rules require use of the DSS."

On 13 December, 1993 IBM announced the sale, effective 1 January, 1994, of IBM Federal Systems Company to the Loral Corporation for $1.575 billion in cash. IBM Federal Systems Marketing, which sells standard IBM products and services to government agencies, is not part of the transaction. IBM Federal Systems Company had revenues of $2.1 billion in 1992, and $2.3 billion in 1993. Approximately 60% of the unit's business is with military and intelligence customers, with the remaining 40 percent consisting of systems integration contracts for other federal agencies such as the US Postal Service and the Federal Aviation Administration (FAA).

In addition to the CIA, other Lotus Notes customers include the Drug Enforcement Administration, the Federal Bureau of Investigation, the Defense Intelligence College, the Defense Mapping Agency (DMA), the National Security Agency (NSA), and the Defense Intelligence Agency (DIA).

IDG [Infovision]
International Data Group
International Data Corporation
IDC Government [Infovision International]
3110 Fairview Drive
Suite 1100
Falls Church, VA 22043

International Data Group (IDG) is a leading global provider of information services on IT, with more than 8,000 employees in 68 countries.

International Data Corporation (IDC) is the leading provider of market information, industry analysis, and strategic and tactical guidance to builders, providers, and users of information technology.

IDC Government is a research and advisory services company that helps government agencies by providing independent analysis of information technology issues for sound decision making. IDC Government services are tailored to meet the unique IT needs of commercial and military clients, including the Office of Naval Intelligence.

Ilex Systems, Inc.
1838 Paseo San Luis
Sierra Vista, AZ 85635

Ilex Systems maintains the software on the Army's All Source Analysis System (ASAS), all army intelligence collection systems and weather and terrain systems. Ilex has 75 field software engineers (most former intelligence officers or NCO's) located wherever ASAS has been fielded by the army.

I-NET
Headquarters
6700 Rockledge Drive
Bethesda, MD 20817
http://www.inet.com

Other Addresses:

Colorado Springs, CO

On 14 December, 1995 Betac was awarded one of two contracts with a combined $120 million ceiling by the US Air Force Space Warfare Center, Colorado Springs, CO, under the Tactical Exploitation of National Capabilities (TENCAP) program. The Betac team includes I-NET. The initial tasks under the Space Warfare Center Operations Support Contract (SWCOSC) will be to provide education and training support and systems planning support to enhance combat operations by integrating national and Department of Defense space systems into command and control warfare (C2W), intelligence, and warfighting capabilities. Additional tasks covered under the contract include support to the SWC in the areas of requirements analysis, contingency support, and modeling and simulation to support Special Access programs.

Information Technology & Applications
1875 Campus Commons Drive
Reston, VA 22091

Other Addresses:

    Colorado Springs, CO

Information Technology and Applications Corporation, an employee-owned business with $10 million in annual sales, provides satellite communications and graphical fusion display hardware and software design integration for the military services and classified agencies.

On 22 November, 1995 ITA was awarded one of two Space Warfare Center Operations Support Contracts (SWCOSC)—the other going to Betac—with a value of $68,180,000 by the US Air Force Space Warfare Center, Colorado Springs, CO, under the Tactical Exploitation of National Capabilities (TENCAP) program for engineering and technical services to improve the ability of combat forces to utilize space and national systems.

Infosystems Technology, Inc.
6411 Ivy Lane
Greenbelt, MD 20770

This privately-held company was founded in 1976 and currently has sales of less than $1 million with the TRUSTED RUBIX(tm) relational database software and other secure UNIX systems services.

Infotech Development Inc.
3611 South Harbor Blvd.
Santa Ana, CA 92704

Intergraph USA
Headquarters
Huntsville, AL 35894-0001
http://www.ingr.com/usa/index.html

Other Addresses:

Utilities and Mapping Sciences Division

Federal Systems Division

Regional Training Center, 12347-B Sunrise Valley Drive, Reston, VA 22091

2051 Mercator Drive, Reston, VA 22091

Intergraph is a billion-dollar, Fortune 500 company that develops and sells software, hardware, and services for technical professionals, particularly those in computer aided design, manufacturing and engineering [CAD/CAM/CAE] and geographic information systems [GIS] disciplines. The company offers open solutions, including software for the Windows and UNIX environments and Intel-based personal workstations and symmetric multiprocessing servers. Employing 9,000 people, the company has offices in more than 50 countries in the Americas, Europe, the Middle East, and Asia-Pacific. Total revenues for 1994 were $1.04 billion, down 1% for the year after an 11% decline in 1993 and a 2% decline in 1992. Sales of Intergraph systems in 1994 were $665.6 million, down 1% after declines of 15% and 8%, respectively, in the two preceding years.

The architecture, engineering, and construction (AEC), mapping/geographic information systems (GIS), and mechanical design, engineering, and manufacturing (MDEM) product applications have dominated the Company's product mix, with the relative contributions of these product families to total systems revenue for both 1994 and 1993 were AEC 34%, GIS 42%, MDEM 16%, and all other applications 8%.

Intergraph Federal Systems markets commercial off-the-shelf products, as well as specially developed products and services, and the company is the leading provider of interactive computer graphics systems to the federal government, including federal mapping operations and services, as well as system design and integration in the intelligence arena and international mapping. Total systems and maintenance and services revenue from the United States government was approximately $167 million in both 1994 and 1993 and $186 million in 1992 (16% of total revenue in each of the three years), including system support contract and other work for the Defense Mapping Agency. The company is also working on the Terrain Feature Generator (TFG) system to support weapons system target location and tracking decisions.

Intermetrics
Corporate Office
733 Concord Ave.
Cambridge, MA 02138
http://www.inmet.com

Other Addresses:

800 K Street, N.W. Suite 830, Washington, D.C. 20001

7918 Jones Branch Drive, Suite 710, McLean, VA 22102

3104 Timanus Lane, Suite 209, Baltimore, MD 21244

Intermetrics is a world-class software development and systems services company that for over 25 years has provided its customers with information technology solutions providing security systems engineering and integration, requirements analysis, and accreditation support. The Systems and Software Services Division is comprised of Intermetrics Systems Services Corporation (ISyS) and the Information Systems Department. The Information Systems Department is responsible for business related to information systems and systems security support.

On 1 December, 1995 the Air Force Electronic Systems Center awarded a five-year $929 million contract for the Integration for Command, Control, Communications, Computers and Intelligence (IC4I) program to BTG and Cordant. This small-business set-aside procurement will supply the intelligence community with hardware, software and integration services focused on manufacture and development of interoperable systems and subsystems to upgrade the Intelligence Data Handling System and other systems. BTG's principal teammates are EDS, Intermetrics, and Sterling Software Inc.

ITT Corporation

ITT Corporation
ITT Industries
ITT Defense & Electronics, 1650 Tysons Boulevard, Suite 1700,
McLean, VA 22102
ITT Federal Systems

Created in 1920 as a telephone operating company in the Caribbean, ITT
grew into a unique company on the international business scene—
International Telephone & Telegraph— later to be known simply as ITT.
In the late 1960s and through the '70s, ITT acquired more than 250
companies including Avis Rent-A-Car, Continental Baking Company,
Canteen, Rayonier, Sheraton, Hartford Fire Insurance Company, and
others. In 1986, in one of the most important business transactions of the
decade, ITT, then $24 billion in sales and revenues, exited its foundation
business with the sale of 63% of its telecommunications operations into
a joint venture with Alcatel Alsthom (CGE of France). ITT successfully
became a more focused multinational giant with service and manufacturing operations in over 100 countries around the globe. In addition, since
the 1986 sale of the telecommunications business, ITT rebuilt its sales
and revenues to the $25 billion level and the market equity value of ITT
has nearly tripled from $5 billion to some $13 billion.

On 13 June, 1995 ITT Corporation approved a management plan to
spin-off its businesses to shareholders to create three separate publicly
owned corporations. The transaction, involving sales and revenues of
some $25 billion, is one of the largest of its kind in business history. The
three independent companies are: ITT Hartford, the current insurance
business of ITT; the new ITT Corporation, made up of ITT Sheraton
Corporation, ITT's interest in CIGA, Caesar's World Inc., ITT's interest
in Madison Square Garden, ITT World Directories, Inc., and ITT's
interest in ITT Educational Services, Inc., and ITT Industries, Inc., the
current automotive, defense and electronics and fluid technology
businesses of ITT.

ITT Industries, comprised of ITT Automotive, ITT Defense &
Electronics and ITT Fluid Technology, designs and manufactures a wide
range of industrial products. ITT Industries generated 1994 sales totaling
$7.6 billion and operating income of $418 million.

ITT Defense & Electronics companies develop, manufacture and
support high technology electronic systems and components for defense
and commercial markets on a worldwide basis, with operations in North

America, Europe and Asia. Defense market products include tactical communications equipment, electronic warfare systems, night vision devices, radar, space payloads, and operations and management services. Commercial products include interconnect products (such as connectors, switches and cable assemblies) and night vision devices. With annual sales of $1.7 billion, ITT Defense & Electronics companies have approximately 14,700 employees in 74 facilities in 15 countries.

Jaycor
Headquarters
9775 Towne Center Drive
San Diego, CA 92121
http://www.jaycor.com

Other Addresses:

1608 Spring Hill Road, Tysons Corner, VA

JAYCOR was founded in 1975 as an advanced technology company to provide services to government and industrial clients. It is a privately held company with 567 employees in offices in 12 cities and sales of $58M. The corporate headquarters is located in San Diego, California, with a major office located in Tysons Corner, VA. Telecommunications engineering, defense sciences and systems development represent the largest business sectors.

J.G. Van Dyke & Associates [VDA]
6550 Rock Spring Drive
Suite 360
Bethesda, MD 20817
http://www.jgvandyke.com

J.G. Van Dyke & Associates, incorporated in 1978 with $15 million annual revenue and 200 professional staff, applies leading edge tools and techniques to provide business-focused solutions in the areas of enterprise system networking, integration, and information security for DoD, the intelligence community, and civilian agencies.

Johns Hopkins Applied Physics Laboratory [JHU APL]
Laurel, MD 20723
http://www.jhuapl.edu

The Applied Physics Laboratory is a not-for-profit research and development division of The Johns Hopkins University dedicated to solving urgent problems of national and global interest. While focused primarily on U.S. Navy and defense tasks, the Laboratory also conducts major programs for civil federal agencies, primarily in space science for NASA, and continues to make contributions in civilian sectors, where national needs are in concert with our capabilities. With more than 140 experimental laboratories and facilities, APL is recognized for its expertise in research, analysis, simulation and modeling, design, prototype development, and test and evaluation. The JHU APL is located just off of Maryland Route 29 on 365 acres, halfway between Baltimore, MD, and Washington, DC. The campus-like grounds include over 40 buildings housing more than 140 specialized laboratories and facilities. Staffed by 2500 people [60% are scientists and engineers] APL's funding level of approximately $400 million is maintained through more than 200 separate tasks and various sponsors, which according to the Baltimore Sun include the National Security Agency.

James Martin Government Intelligence [JMGI]
4350 North Fairfax Drive
Arlington, VA 22203

JMGI, with $3 million in annual sales, provides business process, information engineering and computer systems for law enforcement, intelligence and military agencies.

Jet Propulsion Laboratory
Pasadena, CA
http://www.jpl.nasa.gov

The Jet Propulsion Laboratory is a Federally Funded Research and Development Center [FFRDC] operated for NASA and other government agencies by the California Institute of Technology. The Jet Propulsion Laboratory is the lead U.S. center for robotic exploration of the solar system. JPL spacecraft have visited all known planets except Pluto (a Pluto mission is currently under study for the late 1990s). In addition to its work for NASA, JPL conducts tasks for a variety of other federal agencies. JPL's main 72-hectare (177-acre) site is at the foot of the San Gabriel Mountains near Pasadena, California, 19 kilometers (12 miles) northeast of Los Angeles.

JPL work for the Department of Defense has included the Miniature Seeker Technology Integration (MSTI), a satellite built and launched in November 1992 to demonstrate miniature sensor technology and a rapid development system. JPL also managed the All Source Analysis System (ASAS) project, a battlefield information management system.

Keane Inc.
Corporate Headquarters
Ten City Square
Boston, MA 02129
http://www.keane.com

Other Addresses:

Keane Federal Systems, 1375 Piccard Drive, Rockville, MD 20850

Keane Federal Special Projects, 9710 Patuxent Woods Drive, Columbia, MD 21046

Keane is a software services company that designs, develops, and manages software for corporations and healthcare facilities. Keane Federal Systems helps Fortune 500 companies and the Federal Government by aligning their information systems with changing business and mission objectives. Keane is the largest and fastest growing software services company in its market segment with more than 4,000 technical and business professionals and a network of 40 branch offices throughout North America.

Klassic Concepts Inc.
4813 Lake Hurst Drive
Waco, Texas 76710
http://members.aol.com/sanjuana/HOMEPAGE.HTML

Klassic Concepts provides business development consulting and product marketing representation to commercial, defense, intelligence and law enforcement companies. Services include business development and product representation, assistance in development of proposals and statements of work, independent technical and cost proposal evaluation, creation of short and long range product marketing plans, development of presentations for technical and marketing briefings, training plans and present technical training, and preparation of export licensing briefings. Customers include Lockheed Martin Aircraft Service for Special Missions Aircraft.

LGA Inc.
12500 Fair Lakes Circle
Suite 130
Fairfax, VA. 22033

LGA is a small high-tech consulting firm with expertise in end-to-end planning of experiments, development of measurement instruments, and data analysis in image understanding and related fields, including user needs assessment and requirements gathering, evaluation of Automated Target Recognition algorithms, and development of GUI guidelines for imagery systems for the National Photographic Interpretation Center.

Litton Industries Inc.
Litton Headquarters
360 North Crescent Dr.
Beverly Hills, CA 90210

Other Addresses:

Litton Command, Control and Communications Systems Group

PRC 1500 Planning Research Center Drive, McLean, VA 22102

12005 Sunrise Valley Dr., Reston, VA 22091

1760 Business Center, Reston, VA

2121 Crystal Drive, Arlington, VA

1235 Jefferson Davis Highway, Arlington, VA

4301 North Fairfax Drive, Rosslyn, VA

4401 Ford Avenue, Alexandria, VA

Litton Industries, Inc. is mainly a high-technology aerospace/ defense corporation which provides advanced electronic and defense systems and marine engineering and production to US and world markets. The Company also provides electronic components and interconnect products to customers worldwide. Litton was founded in California in 1953 and has evolved into a major international organization with approximately 29,000 employees at more than 20 major divisions, with annual sales of $3.4 billion.

Litton's ITEK ["Information Technology"] Optical Systems Division performs contract research and development for government customers, and is a leading supplier of imaging and image-processing equipment. With annual sales of over $50 million, 750 employees are housed in 270,000 square feet of facilities in Massachusetts, with support for fielded systems conducted from the Sunnyvale location.

On 15 November, 1995 Hughes Electronics announced plans to acquire the ITEK Division. Approximately 75% of ITEK's 270 employees will be moved to Hughes Danbury Optical Systems division, and the ITEK Lexington facility with be closed.

In December 1995 Litton purchased PRC from Black and Decker for $425 million. PRC was established as Planning Research Corporation in Los Angeles, California. Its first contract is to provide operations research work for the US Army. In 1978 Planning Research Corporation headquarters moved to Washington, D.C. and in 1991 Planning Research Corporation and Advanced Technology, Inc. merge to form PRC Inc., a subsidiary of Black & Decker. PRC has provided scientific and technology-based systems, products and services to government and commercial clients around the world for more than 40 years. The company employs about 7,000 people in more than 200 offices. Revenue increased 15 percent from $761 million in 1993 to $883 million in 1994. PRC is ranked in the top 10 federal information technology contractors, and is the 14th largest employer in the Washington, D.C. region (including suburban Virginia and Maryland).

PRC contracts include work on the Intelligence and Planning (I&P) component of the Advanced Research Projects Agency's (ARPA) War Breaker Program, and the Integrated Tactical Warning and Attack Assessment Sensors Integrated System Support (ISISS) program, as well as other work developing space and intelligence systems.

Lockheed-Martin
Headquarters
6801 Rockledge Drive
Bethesda, MD 20817
http://www.lmco.com

Other Addresses:

Aeronautics Sector, 6801 Rockledge Drive, Bethesda, MD 20817

Lockheed Martin Advanced Development Company [Skunkworks], Palmdale, CA

Space & Strategic Missiles Sector, 6801 Rockledge Drive, Bethesda, MD 20817

Astronautics, Denver, CO 80201

Missiles & Space, Sunnyvale, CA

Technical Operations, Sunnyvale, CA

Westfields, Chantilly, VA

Information & Technology Services Sector, 6801 Rockledge Drive, Bethesda, MD 20817

Management & Data Systems, Valley Forge, PA

Information Systems & Technologies, 640 Freedom Business Center, King of Prussia, PA 19406

Management & Data Systems, 10803 Parkridge Blvd., Reston, VA 22091

Customer System Support Center / MATRIX Program Management Office, 8520 Cinderbed Road, Gateway 95 Business Park, Newington, VA

Springfield, VA

12999 Deer Creek Canyon Road, Denver, CO 80127

Data, Development, and Dissemination (D3) Organization, Austin, TX 78760

Loral Headquarters, 600 Third Avenue, New York, New York 10016

Loral Western Development Labs, 3200 Zanker Road, San Jose, CA 95134

Unisys Paramax, 8540 Cinderbed Road, Gateway 95 Office Park, Newington, VA

Loral Western Development Labs, Research and Development Technology Center, 7100 Standard Drive, Hanover, MD 21076

Loral [ex IBM] Federal Systems Company, 6705 Rockledge Drive, Bethesda, MD 20718

Loral [ex IBM] Federal Systems Company, Loral/IBM Park, 9500 Godwin Drive, Manassas, VA, 22110

Space Imaging, Inc. 9351 Grant Street, Suite 500, Thornton, CO 80229

Lockheed Martin Corporation was formed on 15 March 1995, with the merger of two of the world's premier technology, companies, Lockheed Corporation and Martin Marietta Corporation. Headquartered in Bethesda, Maryland, Lockheed Martin is a leader in the aerospace industry with core businesses in aeronautics, electronics, energy and environment, information and technology services, materials, space systems, launch vehicles and missiles. It employs approximately 165,000 people worldwide, and had sales of $23 billion in 1994. Lockheed-Martin has purchased a 28.4 acre site adjacent to the NRO Headquarters Westfields business park and is awaiting construction of new buildings.

In April 1993, Martin Marietta Corporation consummated a transaction in which its businesses and the Aerospace businesses of the General Electric Company (GE) were combined. And on 22 December, 1993 Martin signed an agreement with General Dynamics to purchase its Space Systems Division, including the Atlas series of space launch vehicles.

Established as a separate entity in 1990, Lockheed Advanced Development Company was formed from Lockheed's Advanced

Development Projects organization, known throughout the aerospace industry as the Skunk Works, which previously operated as a unit of a larger Lockheed division. After 50 years in Burbank, Calif., Skunk Works headquarters relocated to Palmdale at the end of 1992. The company has now transferred all of its operations to Antelope Valley. Its base of operations is the 542-acre Lockheed Martin Plant 10. The Skunk Works property is adjacent to U.S. Air Force Plant 42 at Palmdale. Lockheed Martin test flights use Plant 42's runways. By 1995 the company-owned Plant 10 complex incorporated some 45 buildings housing about 2.2 million square feet of floor space. Another 52,000 square feet of leased office space nearby is also being utilized. In addition, Skunk Works personnel perform modification and systems upgrade work on U-2 and F-117 aircraft at two government-owned sites at Air Force Plant 42. At the beginning of 1995, the company had almost 4,000 employees working in the Antelope Valley.

Products and technologies at Lockheed Martin Astronautics are organized under eight distinct areas: Space Launch Systems, which includes current Titan II and IV expendable launch systems and related business; Space Systems, which includes Atlas and Centaur launch systems as well as the Multi-Service launch System (MSLS); Advanced Launch Systems, which includes development of the next generation of space boosters Ground Systems, which is responsible for Department of Defense (DoD), Department of Energy (DoE) and National Aeronautics and Space Administration (NASA) ground system programs; Flight Systems, which is responsible for space systems programs, Advanced Interceptor Technology and Peacekeeper programs; and Special Programs and Defense Systems, which are involved in various classified government programs.

Astronautics occupies several campuses in the south and southwest suburbs of Denver, Colorado and one in Colorado Springs, 70 miles south of Denver. The Deer Creek Facility, Astronautics headquarters, is located about 20 miles southwest of downtown Denver at the foot of the Rocky Mountains. This facility includes 711,000 square feet of office space and resides on 1,060 acres in Deer Creek Canyon. The company's main facilities house research, production and manufacturing capabilities, and are located on 5,400 acres of foothills about five miles southwest of the Deer Creek offices. This $550 million campus offers some of the most sophisticated production, space simulation and test facilities in the world, and includes more than 70 modern laboratories and several hundred thousand square feet of computerized engineering design, advanced manufacturing and administrative capabilities.

The company also operates United States Air Force launch facilities for the Titan and Atlas launch vehicle programs at Vandenberg Air Force Base, California, and Cape Canaveral Air Station, Florida. There are also Astronautics facilities in San Diego, California, and in Harlingen, Texas.

The Information and Technology Services Sector provides command and control systems, information processing services, systems engineering, integration, program management, software development, computer-based simulations and training products, computer-based test control, machinery control, and automated logistics systems to civil, military and commercial customers.

Founded in 1991 as the GE Advanced Concepts Center, the Center became Martin Marietta Information Systems & Technologies (IS&T) as part of a 1993 merger of Martin Marietta Corporation and GE Aerospace. Today it is a key component of Lockheed Martin Management & Data Systems (M&DS), a $1 billion, six thousand employee company of the Lockheed Martin Corporation. M&DS has a 30-year tradition of providing integrated information solutions and services to a growing government and commercial market.

The Data, Development, and Dissemination (D3) Organization includes 900 employees working in 400,000 square feet of computer laboratories, offices, and high-bay manufacturing facilities on a 700 acre campus. Special Programs include systems and software development/ integration of ground control processing, image and map processing, signal processing, communication and message handling, and other specialized systems.

The Space & Strategic Missiles Sector and the Information & Technology Services Sector are headquartered in Bethesda, MD. The company is engaged in a number of classified programs, and the results of operations related to those programs are included in the company's consolidated financial statements.

The Space and Strategic Missiles Sector includes Lockheed Martin Missiles & Space, a major aerospace and defense company specializing in the development of space systems, missiles and other high technology products since it was founded in 1954. Missiles & Space employs 14,000 workers nationwide with more than 9,500 employees in the San Francisco Bay Area. The Space Systems Division (SSD) develops and integrates nationally critical satellites and ground systems for defense, civil space and science purposes. It serves as the prime integration, systems production and launch contractor to the US Air Force for the Titan series of expendable space launch vehicles. These include the Titan II, Titan III and Titan IV. Data, Development, and Dissemination (D3) Organization activities in Austin, TX include the Softcopy Mapping System (SMS), image and signal processing systems.

On 8 January, 1996 Lockheed Martin Corporation and Loral Corporation announced agreement on the combination of the two companies' defense electronics and system integration businesses. Lockheed Martin will acquire Loral's defense electronics and system integration businesses, including the former IBM Federal Systems Company, for approximately $9.1 billion. When the transaction is complete, Lockheed Martin's annual combined sales will reach approximately $30 billion with a total backlog of approximately $47 billion. The company will operate with a discretionary research and development budget of approximately $1 billion per year, and is expected to generate approximately $1.5 billion to $2.0 billion in free cash annually. Lockheed Martin currently is organized in five business sectors: Aeronautics, Electronics, Energy & Environment, Information & Technology Services, and Space & Strategic Missiles. When this transaction is completed, the Loral business units initially will constitute a sixth sector, Tactical Systems. A long-term consolidation plan will be developed following thorough review and analysis to determine how to best integrate these businesses.

Loral Corporation was incorporated in New York in 1948, and through its subsidiaries and divisions is a leading supplier of advanced electronic systems, components and services to US and foreign governments for defense and non-defense applications. Loral's principal business areas are: electronic combat; training and simulation; tactical weapons; command, control, communications and intelligence (C3I)/ reconnaissance; systems integration; and telecommunications and space systems. During fiscal 1995, sales increased to $5.484 billion from $4.009 billion in the prior year. Substantially all of the Company's products are sold to agencies of the US Government, primarily DoD, to foreign government agencies or to prime contractors or subcontractors thereof. In fiscal 1995, approximately $4.32 billion of the Company's sales was directly or indirectly from United States and foreign government defense contracts and approximately $991 million was directly or indirectly from U.S. and foreign government non-defense contracts. At March 31, 1995, the Company employed approximately 28,900 persons.

LORAL Western Development Labs, is one of the leading system developers and system integrators for the Intelligence Community.

Loral's guidance programs include the Digital Scene Matching Area Correlation (DSMAC) guidance system for the Tomahawk cruise missile. Loral offers systems integration, operations management and engineering services, post-deployment systems support, military satellite communication terminals, information processing and display hardware, information management software, secure tactical communications instruments and telemetry equipment to address a broad spectrum of strategic and tactical

C3I requirements. Loral is developing the communications element of the All-Source Analysis System, a tactical intelligence fusion system.

In July 1990 Loral purchased the Aerospace Division of Ford Motor Co., whose assets included the Western Development Labs, whose Hannover, MD Center is, according to the Baltimore Sun, a contractor to the National Security Agency.

Effective 1 January, 1994, Loral Federal Systems Company ("LFS"), acquired from IBM the Federal Systems Company, headquartered in Bethesda, MD, a leading systems integrator and supplier of advanced information technology products and services to defense and non-defense government agencies worldwide.

On 5 May, 1995 Loral acquired the Defense Systems operations of Unisys Corporation. Unisys Defense Systems ("Loral UDS") is a leading systems integrator and supplier of advanced information technology products and services to defense and other government agencies worldwide. Loral UDS is a technology leader in high data rate, covert, jam-resistant microwave communications in support of core military and other national agency reconnaissance and surveillance applications. Loral's EMR and instrumentation telemetry systems include airborne transmitters, receivers, data links, transponders and signal encoders, which are used in tracking, ranging, data acquisition and command and control for operations of space vehicles and missiles. Loral's instrumentation products, primarily the System 500, provide high-speed, real-time processing in testing and analyzing data from advanced avionics, as well as from missile and satellite sources. Loral, as systems prime contractor, is utilizing its sensing and imaging products as major components of the Advanced Tactical Air Reconnaissance System (ATARS) and the Long-Range Oblique Photography System (LOROPS).

Lockheed Martin Tactical Defense Systems was formerly known as Loral Defense Systems-East. Prior to that it was a division of Unisys Corporation, and has also been known as Paramax. It is one of three prime contractors on the STARS program. Some papers and newsletter articles refer to the former identities for Lockheed Martin Tactical Defense Systems. The Loral Defense Systems STARS team is partnered with the Army for usage of Software Technology for Adaptable, Reliable Systems (STARS) product line approaches/technologies in a real-world context. Army CECOM is applying STARS technologies in the Reengineering of an Intelligent Electronic Warfare (IEW) system— Guardrail Common Sensor 4 (GRCS4) and establishing a reuse base within IEW beginning with the domain of Emitter Location, Processing and Analysis (ELPA). The Lockheed Martin Tactical Defense Systems STARS team, currently composed of Lockheed Martin Tactical Defense

Systems, Organon Motives, CTA, ASR and TRW, have worked together to develop/integrate a technology base supporting domain-specific reuse and process driven development. Lockheed Martin Tactical Defense Systems is partnered with Hewlett-Packard (HP) as a commercial counterpart—HP technology provides the base framework onto which STARS technologies are integrated.

Logicon Inc
Logicon Headquarters
3701 Skypark Dr.
Torrance, CA 90505

Other Addresses:

Logicon, 1815 N Lynn St., Arlington, VA 22209

Logicon, 1831 Wiehle Avenue, Reston, VA 22090

Logicon Eagle Technology, 265 1/2 Fraley Boulevard, Dumfries, VA

Logicon RDA, 6940 S Kings Hwy., Alexandria, VA 22310

Logicon Ultrasystems, 14175 Sullyfield Circle, Suite 700, Chantilly, VA 22021

Logicon Ultrasystems, 155 Moffest Park Dr., Sunnyvale, CA 94089

Logicon was founded in 1961. Since that time, the company has experienced a steady rate of growth and profitability, both of which have significantly accelerated in the last ten years. Today Logicon, with over 80 offices across the United States and in Western Europe, employs about 5,000 people and enjoys a revenue base of nearly $500 million. The company is organized into four groups, each with a specialized market focus.

Logicon's work includes the Central Imagery Office's National Imagery Transmission Format Standards (NITFS). Logicon Ultrasystems provides system engineering and software development for space systems.

ManTech Advanced Systems International, Inc
Columbia, MD

ManTech Advanced Systems has a $17 millions time and material contract for repair/return maintenance for equipment in the SIGINT Service Center at Fort Meade, Maryland

---

McDonnell Douglas Aerospace
St. Louis, MO 63166
http://www.mdc.com

Other Addresses:

Space and Defense Systems, 11242 Waples Mill Road, Suite 300, Fairfax, VA 22030

The core business of McDonnell Douglas Aerospace (MDA) is the development and production of tactical aircraft, missiles, and space systems for the United States Government, which produce annual revenues of over $13 billion. These complex products require the development and integration of key technologies and processes in order to satisfy customer requirements.

McDonnell-Douglas Space and Defense Systems is focused on military and space weapons systems and command, control, communications and intelligence services. Intelligence-related work includes pattern recognition systems which can recognize complex patterns from a variety of input sources and wavelet-based image compression software which offers state of the art compression of still imagery, providing superior image quality at compression ratios ranging from several to one up to 200:1.

McQ Associates, Inc
1551 Forbes Street
Suite 100
Fredricksburg, VA 22405

Other Addresses:

System Innovations, Inc.

McQ Associates specializes in the design and production of remote sensor systems, including intrusion detection, surveillance, imaging and signal intercept for the military, intelligence and commercial communities. System Innovations, Inc. (SII), a subsidiary of McQ Associates, Inc. founded in 1985, is a high technology firm that specializes in integrated security and surveillance equipment and systems. SII's work has been for a variety of government and commercial customers.

Mead Data Central
9443 Springboro Pike
Miamisburg, OH 45343
http://www.lexis-nexis.com

Other Addresses:

LEXIS-NEXIS, Dayton, Ohio 45401

Mead Data Central, which was purchased in 1994 by Reed Elsevier Inc, provides the LEXIS-NEXIS services, the world's premier Online legal, news and business information services, which are the cornerstone of an array of enhanced information retrieval, storage and document management products and services. Serving customers in more than 50 countries from over 40 sales locations, the company is a division of Reed Elsevier Inc., part of the Reed Elsevier place group, one of the world's leading publishing and information businesses. Reed Elsevier is headquartered in London. LEXIS-NEXIS is based in Dayton, Ohio and employs 4,500 individuals worldwide. LEXIS-NEXIS reported sales of $623 million in 1994, a 13 percent increase from 1993. More than 748,000 active users subscribe to the LEXIS-NEXIS services. There are 6,146 databases between the two services and over 688 billion characters Online. Nearly 2 million documents are added each week to the more than 506 million documents Online.

Merdan Group
Headquarters
4617 Ruffner St.
San Diego, CA 92111

Other Addresses:

1953 Gallows Road, Vienna, VA 22182

The Merdan Group, Inc. is a privately-held California small business specializing in expert security engineering services. Since its incorporation in 1971, Merdan has become a leading security engineering firm in the United States supporting both private industry and the US Government.

MITRE
Headquarters
202 Burlington Road
Bedford, MA 01730
http://www.mitre.org/hometext.html

Other Addresses:

Hanscom AFB, MA

Hayes Building, 7525 Colshire Drive, McLean, VA 22102 (CAASD)

Westgate Building, 1820 Dolley Madison Boulevard

Garfield Building, 1575 Anderson Road

Washington Building, 7798 Old Springhouse Road

Reston Office, 11493 Sunset Hills Road, Reston, VA
Colorado Springs, CO

Ft. Meade, MD
Greenbelt, MD
Suitland, MD
Arlington, VA
Chantilly, VA

The MITRE Corporation is a multifaceted engineering company with offices at numerous locations that provide technical and strategic guidance in information, communications, and environmental systems. MITRE is a nonprofit corporation and is home to Federally Funded

Research and Development Centers (FFRDCs) for both the DoD and the FAA. The MITRE Corporation was formed in 1958 at the request of the US government to provide scientific and engineering services in Command, Control, Communications, and Intelligence Systems [C3I]. MITRE's first task was to help the Air Force develop the nation's first automated, real-time air defense system. Throughout the 1970s and 1980s, MITRE continued to work on air defense and other command, control, communications, and intelligence systems used by Department of Defense clients.

The Center for Advanced Aviation System Development (CAASD) is a Federal Aviation Administration (FAA)-sponsored Federally Funded Research and Development Center (FFRDC).

MITRE has 12 Technical Centers, each devoted primarily to a single technical discipline, including Advanced Information Technologies, Information Security, Network [including National Intelligence Support and the Joint Worldwide Intelligence System], Open Systems [including the Intelligence Center Engineering Laboratory, which provides an evaluation facility for intelligence information systems for both National and Defense intelligence agencies], Sensor and Processing Systems [with work including Joint STARS, HAVE STARE and STEEL TRAP, and other advanced systems], Signal Processing [including signals intelligence and speech processing], and Software. MITRE also maintains an extensive network of laboratories, including the Joint Intelligence Center Laboratory and the National Imagery Transmission Format (NITF) Communications Laboratory, which is located in the Hayes Building.

Motorola
Headquarters
1303 East Algonquin Road
Schaumburg, IL 60196
http://www.mot.com

Other Addresses:

Government and Space Technology Group (GSTG), 8201 E. McDowell Rd, Scottsdale, AZ 85257

Motorola is one of the world's leading providers of wireless communications, semiconductors and advanced electronic systems and services. The company was founded by Paul V. Galvin in 1928 as the Galvin Manufacturing Corporation, in Chicago, Illinois. The name of the company was changed to Motorola, Inc. in 1947. The company is highly decentralized, with four sectors: the Semiconductor Products Sector, the General Systems Sector, the Land Mobile Products Sector, and the Messaging, Information and Media Sector, and two groups: the Government and Space Technology Group, and the Automotive, Energy and Controls Group. Major equipment businesses include cellular telephone, two-way radio, paging and data communications, personal communications, automotive, defense and space electronics and computers. Sales and earnings again set records, with all three of Motorola's major business segments contributing to the continuing growth.

The Group's Government Electronics Division includes the Communications Systems Operation (CSO) engineering and systems integration activities include a wide variety of diverse and highly sophisticated communications products and systems for the military, government agencies and specialized customers worldwide. The Communications Systems Operation, working with the US Army, designed and developed the first Joint Surveillance and Target Attack Radar System (Joint STARS) Ground Station Module (GSM). The Time Critical Targeting Aid [TCTA] is intended to provide the Joint Forces Air Component Commander [JFACC] the ability to hold mobile tactical missile [TM] targets at risk through continuous surveillance and tracking by porting Ground Support Module [GSM] real-time JSTARS moving target indicator and synthetic aperture radar [MTI/SAR] data and other imagery sources [ASARS, SPOT, NITFS] to provide additional intelligence information and dissemination.

The Command, Control, Communications and Intelligence (C3I) business sector of CSO integrates command, control and communications technologies used in special operations, public safety and military applications. The Group's Information Security Operation (ISO), works on systems such as the Network Encryption System and Secure Telecommunication [SECTEL] products Other Group activities are performed by the Tactical Systems Operation (TSO), Radio Systems Operation (RSO), and Government Space Systems Operation (GSSO)

Military Professional Resources Inc. (MPRI)
1201 East Abingdon Drive
Alexandria, VA

Military Professional Resources Inc. (MPRI), with $7 million in annual revenues, provides military training and advice by retired U.S. military officers under contract to foreign governments. Under a contract initiated by a request from the Croatian Defense Minister to US Deputy Secretary of Defense John Deutch the company has played a major role in assisting the Croatian army since the beginning of 1995.

MRJ Inc.
10560 Arrowhead Drive
Fairfax, VA 22030
http://www.mrj.com

With annual sales of $75 million and over 500 employees, MRJ's work includes image and signal exploitation, Geographic Information Systems, parallel computer architecture, performance evaluation, and operating systems and other information management implementations for the military, other federal agencies, and commercial customers.

MTL Systems, Inc.
Headquarters
3481 Dayton-Xenia Road
Dayton, OH 45432-2796

Other Addresses:

11150 Main Street, Fairfax, VA 22030

An employee-owned corporation, MTL Systems, Inc. (MTL) has its headquarters in Dayton, Ohio with office locations in Rome, New York and Washington, D.C. Established in 1955 as Systems Development Corporation and later known as Data Corporation, the company led many photographic science developments and pioneered the migration of photographic processing to digital image processing. The company was acquired by The Mead Corporation in 1967 and operated as Mead Technology Laboratories, Inc. from 1967 until 1981. MTL was acquired by DBA Systems, Inc. from Mead in 1981 and operated as a wholly-owned subsidiary of DBA until 1987 when the employees purchased the assets of the company.

The 100-plus employees of MTL provide the Department of Defense, other governmental agencies and commercial clients with systems and services in the remote sensing, electronic warfare, electro-optical, computer engineering, mapping, reconnaissance and intelligence areas. For more than 30 years, MTL's Advanced Sensor Technologies staff has supported a wide variety of tactical and strategic major reconnaissance imaging systems, through design and production of engineering test targets, real world simulation scenarios, instrumentation and field support of image data collection, as well as sensor system test and evaluation in support of several national programs.

Mystech Associates
5205 Leesburg Pike
Falls Church, VA 22041
http://www.mystech.com

Mystech Associates, Inc. is a twenty-four year old employee-owned, advanced technology company employing over 200 professionals. The company's principal focus is the exploitation of advanced technologies for the development of systems applications in intelligence systems, strategic planning systems, simulation and modeling, knowledge bases, and training.

National Semiconductor Corp [NSC]
Headquarters
Santa Clara, CA
http://www.national.com

Other Addresses:

   10810 Guilford Road, Suite 111, Annapolis Junction, MD 20701

National Semiconductor Corporation (NSC) is the fourth largest US merchant semiconductor manufacturer, and the 12th largest among worldwide semiconductor companies. With annual sales of $2.4 billion, National Semiconductor ranks as number 223 in the Fortune 500 and has 22,400 employees worldwide with nine manufacturing sites spanning the globe.

Nichols Research
Headquarters
4040 South Memorial Parkway
Huntsville, AL 35815
http://www.nichols.com

Other Addresses:

NRC, 1604 Spring Hill Rd, Vienna, VA 22182
NRC, 4141 Colonel Glenn Hwy., Dayton, OH 45431
NRC, 2101 E El Segundo Blvd., El Segundo, CA 90245
CSSi 10260 Old Columbia Road, Columbia, MD 21046

Nichols Research [NRC] was established in 1976 as a professional services company specializing in optical systems used by government agencies. NRC has 22 technical offices that provide direct support to state and federal contracting agencies. In the past 17 years, NRC has grown from a four-person company to over 1000 employees, including nearly 800 professional scientists and engineers.

NRC's Special Programs Business Unit is structured around four general program areas which are linked together and focused by a common thread of intelligence programs. Building on a fifteen year legacy of Intelligence Community program work, ranging from systems engineering to detailed measurements activities to modeling and simulation applications and configuration management for customers such as the National Air Intelligence Center and DIA's Missile and Space Intelligence Center.

NRC's Space Surveillance and Avionics Business Unit designs, tests, and operates systems for space, aircraft, and airborne surveillance/ reconnaissance applications. Personnel expertise includes focal plane technology, optical and reentry materials, cryogenic subsystems, signal processing, and the phenomenology of optical sensing. Founded in 1982, with over 80 employees and $6M in revenues in 1994, Communications & Systems Specialists, Inc. [CSSi] is an information technology firm, specializing in the development of large, distributed, client/server software systems, including SIGINT Systems. CSSi's 15,000 sq. ft. facility with SCIF (Top Secret/SCI) and hardware integration facility provides expertise in all disciplines of the system development process, including systems and software engineering, hardware/software inter-facing, test, configuration management, quality assurance, technical publications, and integrated logistics support.

NAI Technologies, Inc.
7125 Riverwood Drive
Columbia, MD 21046

NAI Technologies supplies field-deployable computers and other systems for digital signal processing, and data acquisition and communications.

Northrop-Grumman
1840 Century Park East
Los Angeles, CA 90067
http://www.northrop.com
http://www.essd.com

Other Addresses:

Advanced Technology & Development Center, 8900 E. Washington Boulevard, Pico Rivera, CA 90660

Military Aircraft Division, One Northrop Avenue, Hawthorne, CA 90250

Data Systems & Services Division, 1111 Stewart Avenue, Bethpage, NY 11714

Electronics & Systems Integration Division, South Oyster Bay Road, Bethpage, NY 11714

Regional Office, Washington, D.C., 1000 Wilson Boulevard, Suite 2300, Arlington, Virginia 22209

Westinghouse Electronic Systems, 1580-A West Nursery Road, Linthicum, MD 21090

Westinghouse Science & Technology Center, 1310 Beulah Road, Pittsburgh, PA 15235

Northrop-Grumman capabilities include airborne and space surveillance, battle management, electronic warfare, and information technologies, along with strategic and tactical aircraft, defense electronics, and precision weapons.

All five Northrop Grumman operating divisions work on aircraft programs, and more than half of the company's revenues in 1994 related to military aircraft. Northrop Grumman's defense electronics business recorded sales, divided among four market areas—surveillance and battle management, electronics and information warfare, electronics and readiness support, and precision weapons. This segment's current business is supplemented by a Northrop Grumman-led team comprising Lockheed-Martin and Harris. The Military Aircraft Division provides extensive structural modifications to the 707s that carry Joint STARS. Northrop Grumman established the Data Systems and Services Division (DSSD) in 1994 to consolidate information services in image processing, high-performance computing, command and control, logistics, and other information needs.

On 3 January 1996 Westinghouse announced that it had signed a definitive agreement to sell its defense and electronic systems business to Northrop Grumman Corporation. Under the agreement, Westinghouse will receive $3.0 billion in cash and Northrop Grumman will assume approximately $600 million in pension and other post retirement liabilities. The defense-related electronic systems business is by far the largest component of Westinghouse's Electronic Systems Group, with 12,000 employees, which will retain several smaller commercial electronic businesses including those serving residential security and telecommunications markets.

The Electronic Systems Group (ESG) provides research, development, production, and support services for electronic systems and subsystems. These systems are developed and manufactured for the Department of Defense, the National Aeronautics and Space Administration, the Federal Aviation Administration, and U.S. allies. ESG has several major divisions equipped and staffed to develop, manufacture, and support many types of systems including fighter and strike avionics, electronic warfare (countermeasures), command and control, space systems, ocean systems, logistics systems, missile launching and handling, marine systems, and missile systems.

The Aerospace Division designs, develops, and produces fire control radar, electro-optical systems, and electronic warfare systems. The Command and Control Division also designs, develops, and produces air traffic control radar, airborne surveillance systems, airspace management systems, communication systems, and surface based radar (land and ship) for surveillance, acquisition, and tracking of airborne targets. The Aerospace and Command and Control Divisions share common and flexible manufacturing facilities, managed by the Manufacturing Operations Division, that are implemented to accommodate the rapid product design change technology. The Manufacturing Operations Division also provides resources and services to manufacture, test, and ensure the quality of produced systems, including material acquisition, fabrication, assembly, test, and inspection.

The Development and Operations Division brings engineering and manufacturing under a single manager to facilitate the transition of research and development to production. The Development and Engineering Divisions concentrate on development of next-generation products and advanced technology insertion for Aerospace Division and Command and Control Division products while providing system engineering and program support for both divisions.

The Advanced Technology Division provides for the development and fabrication of solid-state, microwave, optic, and acoustic technologies in support of other ESG divisions. Design and Producibility Engineering is responsible for product and process design and development for all ESG products

For more than half a century, Westinghouse has been a leader in developing powerful new systems for defense. Core competencies include systems integration, sensor design, development, and production, signal and data processing hardware and software, advanced image processing MMIC, VHSIC, and ASIC design and fabrication, and advanced antenna design.

Westinghouse airborne surveillance and command and control systems include radar and C³I technologies on board AWACS and Joint-STARS aircraft. For more than 25 years, the Westinghouse optical line scan system on the Defense Meteorological Satellite has been beaming down critical weather data to commanders on the ground, and the company continues to explore new materials, techniques, and technologies for space-borne sensing, communications, and exploration. Westinghouse supplies advanced systems for Command, Control, Communications, and Intelligence to the US Department of Defense, integrating systems with sensors, hardware, and software produced by other manufacturers.

A major corporate enterprise, the Science & Technology Center (STC) employs scientists, engineers, and technicians with expert capabilities across a broad range of technologies, including Sytems, Processes and Technologies, Advanced Energy Conversion, and Electronics, Information and Sciences. The Intelligent Systems Department focuses on image and signal recognition systems, including automatic target detection and classification systems with efforts in synthetic aperture radar and signal processing algorithms for recognizing specific target signals in high noise environments.

Northwest Federal Credit Union
http://www.northwestfcu.org

Other Addresses:

> Enterprise, Herndon, VA
> NPIC, Building 213, Washington Navy Yard, Washington, DC
> CIA Old Headquarters Building, Langley, VA
> Plaza Building, Vienna Technology Park, Vienna, VA

The Northwest Federal Credit Union is a non-profit organization operated for Central Intelligence Agency personnel. Those who invest in credit union shares receive liberal dividends. Low interest loans and mortgage loans are also readily obtainable. Loans at an even lower interest rate are available for the purchase of a new automobile. The Credit Union also has Guaranteed Student Loans which are available to students who are employed by CIA. These loans are insured by the Federal Government. Eligibility is not based on family financial status.

Membership consists of:

Personnel assigned or detailed to the Agency and other personnel who work for or with the Agency on a common intelligence mission or project, namely: civilian employees of the Agency; military or civilian personnel of DoD and other US Government agencies or components, contractor personnel, employees of the Credit Union, persons retired as pensioners or annuitants from the Agency, members of their immediate families or widows and widowers of such persons who were joint owners at the time of the member's death.

OAO
Headquarters
7500 Greenway Center
Greenbelt, MD 20770
http://www.OAO.COM

Other Addresses:

> Colorado Springs, CO
> SECON, Inc.

> SECON, Inc. Eastern Division, 702 Russell Avenue, Gaithers-burg, MD 20877

SECON Inc. Western Division, 155A Moffett Park Drive, Suite 101, Sunnyvale, CA 94089

OAO is a privately-held company founded in 1973. It has annual sales of $65 million with over 2,000 employees developing software for engineering, financial analysis and applications development, primarily for US government customers. SECON, Incorporated provides systems engineering for the aerospace industry.

Oracle Corporation
500 Oracle Pkwy
Redwood Shores, CA 94065
http://www.oracle.com

Other Addresses:

3 Bethesda Metro Center, Bethesda, MD 20814

Oracle Corporation is the world's largest vendor of software for managing information, with more than 12,500 software professionals working in 93 countries around the world. On 27 February, 1995 Unisys Corporation and Oracle Corporation announced a renewed Global Alliance Agreement under which Unisys was granted the right to resell the entire line of Oracle products for all hardware and operating system platforms worldwide, with the two companies joining in development, co-marketing, sales, services, and support.

Orbital Sciences Corporation
21700 Atlantic Boulevard
Dulles, VA 20166
http://www.orbital.com

Since its founding in 1982, Orbital has become a world-recognized leader in conceiving and developing innovative space technologies and pioneering business approaches, leading to the design and production of low-cost small space systems. The Company is structured into five autonomous operating groups that focus on specific market areas and technology capabilities, but that also often work together on projects that span two or more of the groups. Orbital has several space-based systems and space-related applications subsidiaries. The organization also features a small corporate staff.

The Advanced Systems Group (ASG) oversees various projects falling outside the scope of OSC's standard launch vehicles and satellite services. These include certain small satellite projects and unmanned aerial vehicles (UAV's). The ASG is located at OSC's headquarters in Dulles, Virginia. From here, members of the ASG have access to management and facilities as needed for project completion.

Orbital's Communications and Information Systems Group (CISG) oversees three subsidiary companies: Magellan Corporation, Orbital Communications Corporation (ORBCOMM), and Orbital Imaging Corporation (ORBIMAGE). ORBIMAGE is dedicated to providing low cost, state-of-the-art remote sensing products and services to customers around the world, including very high spatial resolution imagery with camera tasking availability through OrbView.

Organon Motives
36 Warwick Road
Watertown, MA 02172

The Loral Defense Systems STARS team is partnered with the Army for usage of Software Technology for Adaptable, Reliable Systems (STARS) product line approaches/technologies in a real-world context. Army CECOM is applying STARS technologies in the Reengineering of an Intelligent Electronic Warfare (IEW) system—Guardrail Common Sensor 4 (GRCS4) and establishing a reuse base within IEW beginning with the domain of Emitter Location, Processing and Analysis (ELPA). The Lockheed Martin Tactical Defense Systems STARS team, currently composed of Lockheed Martin Tactical Defense Systems, Organon Motives [which provides software reuse consulting services], CTA, ASR and TRW, have worked together to develop/integrate a technology base supporting domain-specific reuse and process driven development.

ORION Scientific Systems
Headquarters
8400 Westpark Dr.
Suite 200
McLean, VA 22102
http://www.orionsci.com

Other Addresses:

Newport Beach Office, Newport Beach, CA 92658
Johnstown Office, Johnstown, PA

ORION Scientific Systems is a six-year-old software development and consulting firm dedicated to solving complex problems through the application of advanced information technologies, including integrated software packages for the law enforcement and intelligence communities. ORION Scientific Systems Law Enforcement Programs Division has developed a unique set of automated analytic tools called Law Enforcement Analysis Data System [ORIONLEADS]. ORIONLEADS provides a comprehensive approach to the traditional stages of analysis: collection, evaluation, organization, analysis, and dissemination.

Overlook Systems Technologies
1950 Old Gallows Road
Suite 700
Vienna, VA 22182

Overlook provides program and systems management, security systems, and information systems engineering to the government and private sector, with expertise in space and missile systems, and command, control, communications and intelligence.

Pacific-Sierra Research Corp
Corporate Headquarters & Santa Monica Ops
2901 28th Street
Santa Monica, CA 90405
http://www.psrw.com

Other Addresses:

Applied Systems Division, 1400 Key Blvd. Suite 700, Arlington, VA 22209

Dulles Office, 2201 Cooperative Way, Herndon, VA 22071

Pacific-Sierra Research Corporation is an employee-owned company founded in 1971 as an applied research firm. With over 300 employees, PSR has evolved into a $31 million technology company that provides products, services, and analyses to numerous government defense and intelligence agencies, as well as to domestic and foreign commercial clients. PSR's core business areas include information technology applications, high-performance computing, software development, systems inte-gration, and submarine communications. Representative contract work includes defining and analyzing intelligence/operations requirements for airborne and space-based reconnaissance systems, as well as developing concepts of operations for national intelligence support to tactical warfighting units.

Paracel Inc.
80 South Lake Avenue
Suite 650
Pasadena, CA 91101
http://www.paracel.com

Paracel is a three year old start-up in the business of adaptive information filtering systems. It has a unique patented technology, Fast Data Finder® (FDF®) to fine-filter textual data streams at very high speeds. FDF can provide for approximate matching, for example dealing with misspellings and multiple transliterations of names, and is ideal for multiple languages (not only non-English, but also non-Latin, e.g. Kanji & Cyrillic).

Parallax Graphics Inc.
World Headquarters
2500 Condensa Street
Santa Clara, CA 95051
http://www.parallax.com

Other Addresses:

Eastern USA Office, 12110 Sunset Hills Road, Reston, VA

Founded in 1982, Parallax Graphics makes high performance video boards and software for use in a wide range of applications including videoconferencing and collaboration, training, medical imaging, finance, manufacturing, military and intelligence, process control, machine vision, and security.

PixelSoft, Inc.
101 First Street, Suite 429
Los Altos, CA 94022
http://www.pixelsoft.com

PixelSoft, Inc. products include the ISO standard Programmer's Imaging Kernel System Foundation profile Application Program Interface software. PIKS Foundation provides a basic set of software services for image processing software developers, which can serve as building blocks for creating imaging applications in a wide variety of fields including animation, electronic publishing, graphic arts, industrial vision, medical imaging, photo-intelligence, remote sensing and scientific visualization. Pixelsoft's work includes the Central Imagery Office's National Imagery Transmission Format Standards (NITFS).

PRB Associates Inc.
Headquarters
47 Airport View Drive
Hollywood, MD 20636
http://www.prb-cam.com/framed_font.htm

Incorporated in 1977, PRB Associates, Inc. is a privately owned company headquartered in Hollywood, MD on a 13 acre site, roughly six miles from the Naval Air Warfare Center Aircraft Division, Patuxent River. PRB provides a full range of scientific, engineering and technical support capabilities to both the military and industrial communities. Products include the Joint Intelligence Support Tool (JIST), an automated tool that provides the capability to cross reference target and threat information from multiple sources, and the Data Fusion Processor (DFP), which correlates and merges Near Real Time (NRT) parametric and locational database updates into mission planning system databases.

Presearch Inc.
8500 Executive Park Avenue
Fairfax, VA 22031

Nearly $20 million in annual sales. Provides special-purpose and application specific hardware and software systems and services.

Primark
Primark Headquarters,
TASC Corporate Headquarters
55 Walkers Brook Drive
Reading, MA 01867
http://www.tasc.com/about/primark.html

Other Addresses:

TASC, 1101 Wilson Boulevard, Suite 1500, Arlington, VA 22209

TASC, 12100 Sunset Hills Road, Reston, VA 22090

TASC, 14100 Park Meadow Drive, Chantilly, VA 22021

Westfields Corporate Center, Chantilly, VA

TASC, Airport Square 14, Suite 300, 1190 Winterson Road, Linthi-cum, MD 21090

TASC, 4701 Sangamore Road. Bethesda, MD 20816

TASC, Phoenix, AZ

TASC, 55 Walkers Brook Drive, Reading, MA 01867

TASC is a $295M applied information technology company specializing in the development and integration of advanced information systems and services. Founded in 1966, TASC has over 2,200 employees, and offices in 24 locations.

Value-Added Information Services include open source analysis tools and services for scanning and mining information related to topics of interest to particular clients from distributed real-time and other sources. These tools and services provide time sensitive competitive and economic intelligence, market and technology trends, and special event alerts.

TASC is experienced with imaging sensors, processing algorithms, imagery applications and the exploitation process with an in-depth knowledge of program office engineering methods, planning process, out-years plans for national imaging system infrastructure. The company analyzes technical and programmatic issues associated with evolving systems and technology for imagery collection. processing, dissemination, exploitation, and storage. TASC hosts the National Imagery Trans-mission Format Standards (NITFS) HomePage, and many meetings associated with NITFS take place at the TASC, Reading, MA location.

PSYTEP Corporation
101 North Shoreline Blvd.
Corpus Christi, TX 78401

Pulse Engineering
Headquarters
12220 World Trade Drive
San Diego, CA 92128
http://www.pulseeng.com

Other Addresses:

9051 K Red Branch Road, Columbia, MD 21045

Since 1956 Pulse has been creating and supplying quality, innovative magnetic based components to the world leaders in electronics. Headquartered in San Diego, California, Pulse has 8,300 employees at sales and support locations world wide. The recent purchase of Pulse Engineering by Technitrol Inc. (TNL), Trevose, PA. and the merger with Technitrol's Components Division and the Fil-Mag Group has made Pulse a world leader in magnetic based products and manufacturing capability. Fil-Mag, formed in 1990 by the union of FEE of Ogrelet France and the Filter and Magnetics division of Sprague Electric Co., is a leader in magnetics manufacturing technology and automation.

Quality Systems Inc. (QSI)
4000 Legato Road
Suite 1100
Fairfax, VA 22033

QSI provides intelligence and business information systems engineering services, including information and network engineering.

Questech
7600 Leesburg Pike
Falls Church, VA 22043
http://www.questech.com

Questech provides scientific, engineering and technical software, production and program management services to the military, intelligence and commercial communities, specializing in intelligence and electronic and information warfare.

RAND Corporation
1700 Main Street
P.O. Box 2138
Santa Monica, CA 90407
http://www.rand.org

RAND Washington Research Department, 2100 M Street, N.W., Washington, D.C. 20037

RAND is a nonprofit institution that helps improve public policy through research and analysis. From its inception in the days following World War II, RAND has focused on the nation's most pressing policy problems. Research on national security became the institution's first hallmark. In the 1960s, RAND research and analysis began addressing problems of domestic policy. Project AIR FORCE is one of three national security FFRDCs housed at RAND. The other two are the Arroyo Center, serving the needs of the Army, and National Defense Research Institute, providing research and analysis for the Office of the Secretary of Defense, the Joint Staff, and defense agencies. Major sponsors of RAND National Security Programs research include the Assistant Secretary of Defense (Command, Control, Communications, and Intelligence) and components of the intelligence community. Representative products include Domestic Terrorism: A National Assessment of State and Local Preparedness and Cyberwar and Netwar: New Modes, Old Concepts, of Conflict.

Raytheon
Headquarters
Lexington, MA
http://www.raytheon.com

Raytheon Electronic Systems, Bedford, Mass.

E-Systems 6250 LBJ Freeway, Dallas, Texas 75240

E-Systems EMASS, Inc. 2260 Merritt Drive, Garland, Texas 75041

E-Systems Garland Division, P.O. Box 660023, Dallas, Texas 75266-0023

E-Systems Greenville Division, P.O. Box 6056, Greenville, Texas 75403-6056

E-Systems Engineering Research Associates, Inc., 1595 Springhill Road, Vienna, Virginia 22182-2235

E-Systems Melpar Division, 7700 Arlington Boulevard, Falls Church, Virginia 22046-1572

E-Systems, 141 National Business Parkway, Columbia, MD

HRB Systems Maryland Operations, 800 International Drive, Linthicum, MD 21090

Raytheon Company is a $12 billion international, high technology company which operates in four businesses: commercial and defense electronics, engineering and construction, aviation, and major appliances. Founded in Cambridge, Mass. in 1922 as the American Appliance Company, the company adopted the Raytheon name in 1925.

On 3 April, 1995 Raytheon completed the acquisition of E-Systems of Dallas, TX a $2 billion defense and government electronics company specializing in intelligence, reconnaissance, and surveillance systems, command and control, specialized aircraft maintenance and modification, guidance, navigation and control, communications and data systems. E-Systems is one of the top high technology companies in the world, with nearly 16,000 employees worldwide. The acquisition is the largest in Raytheon's 73-year history. Raytheon's principal business is to design, manufacture, and service advanced electronic devices, equipment, and systems for both government and commercial customers.

E-Systems core business is focused on intelligence, reconnaissance and surveillance. Many of these programs are classified, involving the development or upgrading of sensors, platforms, ground processing and integration of complex systems. E-Systems also has considerable capabilities in large scale image processing and advanced signal processing. E-Systems has strong capabilities in communications and data management technologies, including data storage and retrieval systems, image management and communications networks. In partnership with Lockheed-Martin, E-Systems is using its space imaging expertise to provide high resolution, multispectral satellite imaging data for commercial use.

Among E-Systems key defense electronics programs are the RC-135 and U-2 related reconnaissance and surveillance business, the P-3 airframe refurbishment for the US Navy's Sustained Readiness Program, Command, Communications, and Control (C3), the Cooperative Engagement Capability (CEC) program for the US Navy, the advanced narrow band digital voice terminal and the Commander's Tactical Terminal [CTT]. E-Systems also has capabilities in large scale image processing and advanced signal processing. Digital signal processors, developed by the Garland Division, provide processing power equivalent to several super-computers automatically processing, measuring, and analyzing complex, high-density electronic signals. The Tactical Information Broadcast Service terminal, a long-term program from the Greenville Division, provides a tactical communications link between field commanders.

Since 1947, the US Intelligence Community has relied upon the experience, knowledge and expertise of HRB Systems, a wholly-owned subsidiary of E-Systems, for technological solutions, including C5I and key elements for Ground Based Signal Collection Processing, Analysis and Fusion Systems, as well as sophisticated computer algorithms and parallel computer architectures.

Research Associates of Syracuse
Syracuse, NY
http://www.ras.com:80/ras/ras.htm

Research Associates of Syracuse, Inc. (RAS) was originally founded in 1986 to provide engineering and continuing education to the defense community. RAS and its employees have become well known and respected experts in the areas of radar, avionics, intelligence, and electronic warfare with specialties in custom hardware and software design.

Rockwell
Headquarters
Seal Beach, CA
http://www.rockwell.com/texthome.html

Other Addresses:

Rockwell-Collins, Lafayette Business Park
Rockwell-Collins, Dulles International Center
Rockwell-Collins, Westfields

Rockwell is a major global, diversified, high-technology company with two-thirds of its sales coming from commercial and international markets. The company's role as a defense and aerospace contractor, although diminished in volume, remains a very important part of the company. Since the merger of Rockwell Standard and North American Aviation in 1967, Rockwell has possessed a large commercial business portfolio. In 1973 Rockwell acquired Collins Radio Company, and changed its name from North American Rockwell to Rockwell International. The company has 168 plants and research and development facilities with more than 300 facilities in 48 states and 35 foreign countries including corporate offices in Seal Beach, CA, Pittsburgh, PA, and Washington, D.C.

Santa Cruz Operation, Inc. (SCO)
Headquarters
400 Encinal Street
Santa Cruz, CA 95061
http://www.sco.com

Other Addresses:

Government Systems Group, 2100 Reston Parkway, Suite 102, Reston, VA 22091

SCO is the world's leading provider of system software for Business Critical Servers that run critical day-to-day business operations of large and small organizations, and the leading provider of software that integrates Microsoft® Windows® PCs and other clients with all major UNIX® System servers.

SAIC
Headquarters
1710 Goodridge Drive
McLean, VA 22102
http:www.saic.com

Other Addresses:

1901 North Beauregard Street, Alexandria, VA
2111 Eisenhower Avenue, Alexandria, VA
200 North Glebe Road, Arlington, VA
1213 Jefferson Davis Highway, Arlington, VA
3300 Washington Boulevard, Arlington, VA
4001 North Fairfax Drive, Arlington, VA
5107 Leesburg Pike, Falls Church, VA
5201 Leesburg Pike, Falls Church, VA
505 Huntmar Park Drive, Herndon, VA
11251 Roger Bacon Drive, Reston, VA
SAIC Ideas Group, 7120 Columbia Gateway Drive, Columbia, MD
21046

Science Applications International Corporation provides high-technology services and products to government and the private sector in areas of energy, environment, health, space, and systems integration with annual revenues of $1.7 billion, this employee-owned company has about 17,000 employees in over 350 locations worldwide. Founded by a small group of scientists in 1969, SAIC reported revenues of $1.9 billion for the fiscal year ended 31 January 1995 and ranks as one the largest employee-owned high-tech firm in the nation. The Defense Information Systems Agency has selected SAIC to integrate the Global Command and Control System (GCCS), a global network of fused information systems to support the commanders-in-chief of the unified commands, which will replace the World Wide Military Command and Control System.

SAIC acquired the government sectors of IDEAS, Inc. in November 1994. Now known as the SAIC Ideas Group, this business area encompasses over 230 technical people located in Columbia, Maryland. The SAIC Ideas Group develops, integrates, tests and installs signals intelligence systems. With annual sales of $30 million, its products include digital recorders and adaptive filters, software and hardware design engineering, and space-qualified hardware.

Scientech, Inc.
1690 International Way
Idaho Falls, ID 83402

Scientech supports CIA's Surveillance, Collection and Operations Support subgroup of the Technology Support Working Group, Office of Special Technology, 10530 Riverview Road, Fort Washington, MD 20744

Secure Solutions
9404 Genesee Avenue
Suite 237
La Jolla, CA 92037

Secure Solutions provides information systems security to a variety of customers, including SAIC and the National Security Agency.

SIGTEK Inc.
9821 Broken Land Parkway
Columbia, MD 21046
http://www.sigtek.com/sigtek

SIGTEK designs and manufactures a wide variety of spread spectrum signal generators, demodulators, transmitters, encoder/decoder and frame synchronization devices.

Silicon Graphics Computer Systems
Headquarters
2171 Landings Drive
Mountain View, CA 94043
http://www.sgi.com/Overview/overview.html

Other Addresses:

2011 North Shoreline Blvd., Mountain View, CA 94039

12200-G Plum Orchard Drive, Silver Spring, MD 20904

1420 Springhill Road, Suite 155, West McLean, VA 22102

Cray Research, Inc, Corporate Headquarters, 655 Lone Oak Drive, Eagan, Minnesota 55121   **http://www.cray.com**

Cray Research, Chippewa Falls, WI

Cray Research, 8300 SW Creekside Place, Beaverton, OR 97008

Cray Research, 9480 Carroll Park Drive, San Diego, CA 92121

Cray Research, Suite 1406 222 North Sepulveda Boulevard, El Segundo, CA 90245

Cray Research, Suite 203, 894 Ross Drive, Sunnyvale, CA 94089

Cray Research, Suite 520, 4041 Powder Mill Road, Calverton, MD 20705-3106

Government Marketing and Operations, 1001 G Street, NW, Suite 400 West, Washington, DC 20001

For ten years, Silicon Graphics systems, a compatible family of systems ranging from inexpensive desktop clients to multi-processor database or computer servers, has been used in industrial design, database analysis, visual simulation, energy exploration, and entertainment. Silicon Graphics is among the fastest-growing Fortune 1000 companies. The company's revenue run rate is over $2 billion with a compound annual growth rate of 44 percent over the past six years. The POWER CHALLENGE line of super-computing servers scales from entry-level uniprocessor servers to highly expandable 6.48GFLOP parallel compute servers. Hughes Training, Inc., and Eidetics developed the US Air Force Unit Training Device (UTD) used to train F-16 pilots. The Silicon Graphics Onyx (tm) graphics supercomputer feeds a high-resolution out-the-window visual database to the cockpit displays.

Silicon Graphics and Cray Research announced on 26 February 1996 a merger agreement, pursuant to which Silicon Graphics acquired the outstanding shares of Cray Research. The two companies have a combined revenue run rate of nearly $4 billion. Cray Research, Inc., founded in 1972, is the global leader (two-thirds market share) in the market for large-scale supercomputer systems used in government, industry, and academia. Based in Eagan, Minnesota, Cray Research has approximately

4700 employees worldwide and maintains three strategic business units: Supercomputing Systems, Business Systems, and Government Systems. Cray Research's Engineering, Development, and Manufacturing facilities are located in Chippewa Falls, Wisconsin; Beaverton; and San Diego. The company is the revenue leader for both parallel vector supercomputers and massively parallel processing systems in this high-end, scientific and technical simulation market where systems typically are priced from $2 million to $30 million or more. Cray Research supplies the vast majority of supercomputers used by researchers around the world—over 80 percent of the world's supercomputer-based environmental research sites use Cray Research systems. Nearly all DoE and DoD research labs have at least one Cray Research system.

Space Applications Corp.
Headquarters
200 East Sandpointe Ave.
Suite 200
Santa Ana, CA 92707

Other Addresses:

> Systems & Software Engineering Division, 200 East Sandpointe Ave., Suite 200, Santa Ana, CA 92707

> Systems, Software & Simulation Division, 1310 Orleans Drive, Sunnyvale, CA 94089

> Seattle Operations, Seattle, WA

> C3I Analysis and Engineering Division, 901 Follin Lane, Vienna Technology Park, Vienna, VA 22180

Founded in 1969, this privately-held company currently has over 250 employees at ten locations with sales of nearly $30 million providing on-board and ground-based satellite software services, systems engineering and technical assistance and related C3I services.

Sparta
Headquarters
Huntsville, AL
http://www.huntsville.sparta.com

Other Addresses:

Computer Products Directorate, 7926 Jones Branch Drive, Suite 900, McLean, VA 22102

Secure Systems Engineering Division, Columbia, MD

SPARTA is an employee-owned small business that provides information management, systems engineering, computer aided acquisition, logistics support, and advanced technology meeting a broad national spectrum of Defense and commercial needs. SPARTA's Computer Products Directorate is a developer of real-time and telecommunications systems for C4I, government and commercial applications. SPARTA CPD is a full service integrator and developer of these components, as well as providing custom engineering services.

Spot Image
5, rue des Satellites
BP 4359, F 31030
Toulouse cedex, France
http://www.spot.com/anglaise/welcome.htm

Other Addresses:

Spot Image Corporation (USA), 1897 Preston White Drive, Reston, VA 22091

Spot Image was set up in 1982 by the French Space Agency (CNES) to distribute worldwide, satellite imagery returned by the SPOT earth observation satellite. It has become an unrivaled source of geographic information.

SPOT Image has provided the US DoD with complete satellite image coverage of Bosnia. SPOT is being used by the Defense Mapping Agency to derive and view detailed terrain information for strategic and tactical support purposes. During the Bosnian peace talks, SPOT imagery was merged with other data sources and viewed in PowerSceneä,

Cambridge Research Associates' 3-D viewing software, to assist leaders in visualizing the political boundaries, landcover, and infrastructure of the area.

SRA International

Headquarters
2000 15th Street North
Arlington, VA 22201
http://www.srcorp.com

Other Addresses:

4300 Fair Lakes Court, Fairfax, VA

Systems Research and Applications Corporation is a privately held information technology company founded in 1978, with nearly 1000 employees and annual sales of approximately $100 million, specializing in telecommunications and networks, business Reengineering, systems integration, client/server solutions, computer software development, imaging technology, and intelli-gent information systems and products. Natural language processing is a core SRA technology, whose computational linguists offer expertise in more than a dozen languages. SRA develops intelligent information systems based on natural language and concepts for clients in the military and intelligence communities. The company's products include NameTag, a commercial product adapted from technology originally developed for the intelligence community, that finds, identifies, indexes and interprets proper names of people, places, organizations, and corporations that appear in written texts.

System Research Corporation—SRC

128 Wheeler Road
Burlington, MA 01803

SRC, a ten year old company with $44 million in annual sales, provides information system consulting, reengineering, design, development, integration, migration, and fielding, and related selective outsourcing services. The company also supports Local Area and Wide Area Network Communications (LAN/WAN) and RF communications systems used in major government, military, law enforcement, and private sector appli-cations.

SRI International
Headquarters
333 Ravenswood Avenue
Menlo Park, CA 94025
http://www.sri.com

Other Addresses:

Washington Office, 1611 North Kent Street, Arlington, VA 22209

David Sarnoff Research Center, CN 5300, Princeton, NJ, 08543

SRI International is one of the world's largest contract research firms. Founded in 1946 in conjunction with Stanford University as the Stanford Research Institute, this fully independent incorporated nonprofit organization does not manufacture or market any product, nor is it connected with any manufacturing organization. About 1,000 research projects are under way at any given time; the current volume of contract research is over $200 million per year. Of the staff of 1900, nearly two-thirds are in professional and technical categories. Research at SRI is conducted in three major groups—Engineering Research, Science and Technology, and Business and Policy—each of which is organized into divisions and laboratories. The Washington Office is responsible for Department of Defense and Intelligence Community Programs. The DOD and Intelligence Community Programs Organization works with new and existing clients to help analyze their problems, define requirements, and develop innovative approaches using latest state-of-the-art technologies. This organization draws on the technical resources of SRI's Engineering Research, Science and Technology, and Business and Policy Consulting Groups in determining the best approaches to solving client problems. Key client communities include all DOD and Intelligence Community agencies as well as industry.

The David Sarnoff Research Center is a leader in electronic imaging, with expertise in software and digital IC design, process and materials research, digital signal processing hardware and software. Originally it was established as RCA Laboratories in 1942, but after RCA was sold to General Electric in 1986, the Sarnoff Center became part of SRI International, in Menlo Park, CA. In 1993, Sarnoff achieved profitability, a little more than six years after it became a client-supported R&D organization.

Sarnoff work includes high-speed charge couple device [CCD]

imaging electronic cameras and chips, with image chips having very high frame rates (up to 25 times ordinary television frame rate) combined with exceptionally high sensitivity and low noise. Applications include image recording at high speed, multispectral image acquisition, and electro-optical signal processing.

SSDS Inc.
Corporate Headquarters
6595 S. Dayton Street
Suite 3000
Englewood, CO 80111
http://www.ssds.com

Other Addresses:

Baltimore Office, 9841 Broken Land Parkway, Suite 100, Columbia, MD 21046

Colorado Springs Office, 985 Space Center Drive, Suite 340, Colorado Springs, CO 80915

Los Angeles Office, 222 N. Sepulveda Blvd., Suite 1505, Los Angeles, CA 90245

Washington, DC Office, 8150 Leesburg Pike, Suite 1100, Vienna, VA 22182

SSDS creates technology solutions; designing, planning, implementing and managing information infrastructures that assist clients in gaining a competitive advantage in two key service areas: preparing companies for Electronic Commerce; and implementing customer care solutions in an Electronic Commerce world. Headquartered in Englewood, Colorado, the company has approximately 300 employees in 20 offices across the US. In 1995, United Video Satellite Group (UVSG), a diversified satellite communications company, listed on NASDAQ, acquired a 70% interest in SSDS. Since its founding in 1986, SSDS has implemented over 400 successful open systems solutions for customers in a wide range of industries including computer and networking, telecommunications, healthcare, manufacturing, finance, distribution, and government, in-cluding Intelligence Organizations, Special Operations Commands, and Special System Program Offices.

Scientific and Technical Analysis Corp.
11250 Waples Mill Road
Suite 300
Fairfax, VA 22030

With annual sales of $3 million, STAC provides analytical tools and services to the intelligence community, including foreign technology assessment, non-proliferation analysis, collection system development, and satellite simulation and orbital analysis.

Sterling Software
Corporate Headquarters
8080 North Central Expressway
Suite 1100
Dallas, TX 75206
http://www.sterling.com

Other Addresses:

Federal Systems Group (FSG), 1650 Tysons Blvd., Suite 800, McLean, VA 22102

Information Technology Division, 1406 Fort Crook Road South, Bellevue, NE 68005

Washington Office, 1650 Tysons Boulevard, Suite 800, McLean, Virginia 2210

Rome, New York Department, Beeches Technical Campus, Route 26N, Rome, NY 13440

Sterling Software, Inc., the ninth largest software company worldwide, is a worldwide leader in Electronic Commerce, systems software, and government-related professional services. The company employs approximately 2,900 people in over 50 offices worldwide organized into four groups and sixteen divisions to focus on its three key markets and the international marketplace.

Sterling's Federal Systems Group provides highly specialized technical professional services to the federal government. The group's services focus on scientific software support, supercomputer facilities management, graphics and visualization software, virtual reality systems, network systems, automated message handling and secure data communications.

The Information Technology Division of the Federal Systems Group specializes in developing and fielding ADP systems that leverage practical application of leading edge technology for a wide range of Department of Defense and Intelligence agency customers. Experts in distributed computing and legacy system migration, the division empowers its customers to realize their visions of ever improving support to the warfighter. These systems are created in partnership with the customer, from project concept through delivery and life cycle support.

Sun Microsystems
Headquarters
2550 Garcia Ave.
Mt. View, CA 94043
http://www.sun.com

Other Addresses:

Sun Federal, 2650 Park Tower Drive, Vienna, VA 22180

Sun Microsystems, Inc., founded in 1982, is located in the heart of Silicon Valley and employs more than 14,500 people worldwide. For fiscal 1995, company revenues were $5.9 billion and have averaged 15-20 percent growth over the last several years. While the company's legacy has been as a technical workstation supplier, Sun is transforming itself into an enterprise computing firm focused on global network computing. Sun's open computing philosophy dissolved the model of proprietary computing by offering powerful, less expensive computers using off-the-shelf components. The Sun computing platform features SPARC/Solaris technologies, which offer high performance, openness, ease of use and superior networking. While Sun continues to support its Motorola and Intel-based lines, SPARC comprises 100% of shipments.

Sybase, Inc.
Headquarters
6475 Christie Avenue
Emeryville, CA 94608
http://www.sybase.com

Other Addresses:

Government [Federal] Division, 6550 Rock Spring Drive, Suite 800, Bethesda, MD 20817

Sybase, Inc., is a leading vendor of client/server software and services for building on-line, enterprise-wide information systems. Since its founding in 1984, the company has supported the information management needs of major organizations worldwide. With 4,500 employees at 75 offices and 45 distributors in 49 countries, Sybase was, in 1994, the world's fastest-growing and second-largest independent supplier of enterprise client/server relational database products and services.

In August 1995 the Sybase Federal division was renamed the Sybase Government division, responsible for sales to state and local governments in addition to the federal government. This division has 150 employees dedicated to supporting federal customers through telemarketing, business development, and sales support, as well as systems integration, consulting, and education services. Sybase customers are active in all key federal markets—defense, intelligence, and civilian organizations. Other Sybase intelligence community customers include the US Atlantic Command Joint Intelligence Center and the National Photographic Interpretation Center.

Synectics Corp.
10400 Eaton Place
Suite 200
Fairfax, VA, 22030

This privately held company, founded in 1969, has annual revenues of $15 million based on information technology services such as photogrammetric and computer mass storage systems.

Syracuse Research Corp.
Merril Land
Syracuse, NY 13210

This non-profit corporation, with $17 million in annual revenue, provides research and development services in areas such as analysis of satellite communications systems and intelligence community data-bases.

System Planning Corporation
1000 Wilson Boulevard
Arlington, VA 22209
http://www.sysplan.com

Other Addresses:

> SPC Technology Center, 1429 N. Quincy Street, Arlington, VA
> 22207

System Planning Corporation is a systems engineering firm located in
Arlington, Virginia. Its primary areas of business are radar and sensor
system development; federal program support; monitoring systems;
national security studies; and advanced-technology systems. The SPC
Center for Strategic Systems (CSS) is engaged in studies in collaboration
with the intelligence community, academia, and the national laboratories
in modeling, and simulation of the strategic and theater ballistic missile
threats that the United States and its allies face in the post-Cold War era.
Primary SPC intelligence work seeks to establish a framework that allows
for the organization, management, and tracking of many complex
requirements for the purpose of answering specific Key Intelligence
Questions.

Tech-Ed Services, Inc.
5430F Lynx Lane, #308P
Columbia, MD 21044

Tech-Ed has Virginia & Maryland fee-paid openings, SBI & POLY
required, for engineers, including analog/IC design engineers [$55-95K],
DSP design engineers [$55-75K], spacecraft mechanical design [$50-
65K], Internet engineers [$45-85K], airborne SIGINT system engineers
[$55-75K], software and hardware test engineers [$45-65K], INFOSEC
engineers [$55-75K], UNIX/Solaris system administrators [$35-75K],
and LAN/WAN technicians [$28-65K].

3Com Corporation
Headquarters
Santa Clara, CA
http://www.3Com.com

Other Addresses:

Washington Office, 8075 Leesburg Pike, Suite 300, Vienna, VA 22182

3Com's name is derived from its emphasis on COMputer, COMmunication, and COMpatibility. 3Com is a global company with 71 offices located in 30 countries and over 4,500 total employees worldwide, with approximately 2,000 based in the Bay Area. Annual sales were nearly $1.3 billion in fiscal year 1995, and for the first quarter of fiscal 1996. Founded in 1979, 3Com Corporation pioneered the data networking industry. Today, 3Com offers customers a broad range of ISO 9000-compliant global data networking solutions that include routers, hubs, remote access servers, switches and adapters for Ethernet, Token Ring, and high-speed networks. Intelligence community customers include the Defense Mapping Agency, National Security Agency, Central Intelligence Agency, and Defense Intelligence Agency.

Titan Corporation
Headquarters
3033 Science Park Road
San Diego, CA 92121
http://www.titan.com

Other Addresses:

Titan Systems, 1900 Campus Commons Drive, Suite 400, Reston, VA 22091

The Titan Corporation is a leader in providing information systems and services to commercial, international and government clients. Its business is focused in two primary areas: information systems and applied technologies. Titan sells its systems and services across the United States and in more than 30 countries. Founded in 1981, Titan has over 1,000 employees.

The Systems Group continued to pursue and win new defense intelligence contracts. Titan's secure television business provides complete turnkey security for television delivery systems. The Video PassPort® television encryption system provides solutions to the customers' need to guard programming against unauthorized reception while affording instant access to authorized users. The system has applications for delivery of television programming via satellite, coaxial cable, fiber optics and wireless means.

Tracor
6500 Tracor Lane
Austin, TX 78725

Other Addresses

GDE Systems Inc, Rancho Bernardo, San Diego, CA 92186

GDE Systems, Colorado Springs, CO

GDE Systems, Omaha, NE

GDE Systems, St. Louis, MO

GDE Systems, Washington, 1215 Jefferson Davis Highway, Arlington, VA

GDE Systems, 1840 Michael Faraday Drive, Reston, VA

GDE Helava Associates, Inc.

Vitro Corporation, 1601 Research Boulevard, Rockville, MD 20850

GDE Systems Inc., a San Diego based company, is an industry leader for high quality image exploitation systems. The company has a heritage of nearly four decades as a major electronics contractor for DoD as the General Dynamics Electronics Division. GDE has delivered more than 300 systems to domestic and foreign customers. These systems support varied applications, including Mapping, Charting and Geodesy (MC&G), analysis and exploitation, and economic development monitoring.

Major products include the Digital Imagery Workstation Suite (DIWS), the Digital Photogrammetric Workstation, the Intelligence Data Handling System (IDHS), the Joint Service Imagery Processing System (JSIPS-N), MATRIX Multi-Int Exploitation Software, RapidScene Perspective Scene Visualization Real Time Targeting Concept Development (RTT), the SOCET SET - Digital Photogrammetric Workstation, the Terrain Imagery Exploitation System (TIES), and the Tomahawk Strike Coordination Module (TSCM).

Helava Associates, Inc., was formed in 1979 and soon became a sub-contractor to General Dynamics, developing and manufacturing digital photogrammetric workstations for the defense establishment. In 1986, Helava became a subsidiary of General Dynamics with massive contracts in the area of national security. GDE Systems' subsidiary, Helava Associates, Inc., provides integrated digital stereo software for commercial-off-the-shelf hardware. Helava supplies systems to commercial and defense-related customers in international and domestic markets, providing photogrammetric workstations for map compilation, engineering mapping, orthophoto production, digital terrain collection, environmental resource management, and land use identification.

Vitro Corporation is the largest subsidiary of Tracor, providing a range of systems engineering, information engineering and technical services to military, intelligence and commercial customers.

TRW
Headquarters
1900 Richmond Road
Cleveland, OH 44124
http://www.trw.com

Other Addresses:

Space & Defense Sector, 1001 19th Street, North Arlington, VA

Space & Electronics Group (S&EG), One Space Park Redondo Beach, CA 90278

Defense Systems Division, Redondo Beach, CA 90278

Electronics Systems and Technology Division, Redondo Beach, CA 90278

Space and Technology Division, Redondo Beach, CA 90278

Space & Electronics Group, 14110 Sullyfield Circle, Chantilly, VA

Systems Integration Group (SIG), One [12900] Federal Systems Park Drive, Fairfax, Virginia 22033

Systems Integration Group (SIG), 2341 Jefferson Davis Highway, Arlington, VA

Systems Integration Group (SIG), Government Information Services Division (GISD), 12900 Fair Lakes Parkway, Fairfax, VA

Systems Integration Group (SIG), Integrated Engineering Division (IED), 12900 Fair Lakes Parkway, Fairfax, VA

Burlington, MA

Avionics & Surveillance Group (A&SG), One Rancho Carmel, San Diego, California 92128

Avionics & Surveillance Group (A&SG), National Systems, Sunnyvale, California

ESL Incorporated, 495 Java Drive, Sunnyvale, CA 94088

ESL, 1895 Preston White Drive, Reston, VA

TRW Maryland Engineering Laboratory, 9724 Alexander Bell Drive, Columbia, MD, 21046

TRW provides high technology products and services to automotive, space, defense, and information systems and services customers worldwide. Founded in 1901 as the Cleveland Cap Screw Company, the firm made hexagon and square-head cap screws. Capitalizing on the burgeoning automotive and aircraft markets, the company (Thompson Products, Inc., named for its president, Charles E. Thompson) was achieving annual sales in the late 1920s of about $10 million. In the 1950s the company staked out a position in the growing fields of electronics and missiles through an investment in a new Los Angeles firm, the Ramo-Wooldridge Corporation, which in 1958 merged with Thompson Products to form Thompson Ramo Wooldridge, which today is TRW. At that time, annual sales had reached about $400 million. During the 1970s, TRW continued to diversify by acquiring businesses in electro-hydraulics, signal reconnaissance systems, optoelectronics, occupant restraint systems, vehicle components, and information systems. TRW's employment has grown to more than 64,000 with sales of high-technology products and services of $12 billion annually.

The Space & Defense sector consists of space and electronic systems, with 7,300 employees working on projects such as Milstar, Defense Support Program (DSP), and the Tracking and Data Relay Satellites (TDRS); systems integration, with 6,500 employees working on such projects as the Navy's Ocean Surveillance Information System; and avionics and surveillance systems with 3,000 employees working as a key supplier to national intelligence agencies, includes work on signal intelligence systems, such as Senior Smart, DOD's unified Signal Intelligence (SIGINT) system and advanced tactical architecture.

TRW Tactical Systems and TRW National Systems are divisions of Fairfax, VA-based TRW Systems Integration Group. The group performs systems engineering and systems integration, and develops and installs command and control systems, information processing systems, and security systems for federal government agencies, industry contractors, and international customers.

TRW National Systems is a leader in special-purpose digital signal processing systems and intelligence analysis services for the U.S. government. The division has more than 700 employees. TRW National Systems won more than 50 new contracts in 1995 and continued work on more than 50 other contracts. Research and development efforts focused on advanced signal processing technologies and information warfare concepts.

TRW Tactical Systems is a leading supplier of tactical reconnaissance and direction-finding systems to the US military and foreign governments. Research and development efforts center on advanced co-channel signal processing algorithms, and on low-cost imagery intelligence, direction finding, and frequency management systems.

TRW upgraded its Morrison Canyon facility in May 1995 to extend antenna testing to the microwave frequency bands. Located in Fremont, this is one of a few such facilities in the US to accommodate full-scale testing of antenna systems on large vehicles and aircraft on a 360-degree turntable.

TRW's Maryland Engineering Laboratory designs and integrates real-time systems and large signal processing systems using Unix, Fortran and C, along with complex, mathematical and DSP applications.

Unisys
Headquarters
Township Line Road
Blue Bell, PA 19424

Other Addresses:

Federal Systems Division, 8008 Westpark Drive, McLean, VA 22102

7455J New Ridge Rd, Hanover, MD 21076

Township Line & Union Meeting Roads, Blue Bell, PA 19424

Reston, VA

A $7.4 billion company with more than 40,000 employees, Unisys acts as a solutions and system integrator for business and government, complementing those integration skills with a full range of consulting and implementation services, information technology and vertical industry expertise. Unisys Corporation is one of the largest information management consulting companies in the world. Unisys has significant presence in the public sector /government market worldwide. Unisys solutions for the public sector frequently employ key enabling technologies such as imaging and geographic information systems (GIS). Intelligence-related implementations at the Hanover MD location include software migration projects from legacy mainframe to UNIX, and TCP/IP, SNMP, NIS/DIS, UNIX, Lotus Notes, and Windows NT administration. Unisys in Hanover, MD., Northern Virginia, and Johnstown, PA has multiple contracts with both new and ongoing projects integrating UNIX platforms into state-of-the-art LAN/ WAN enterprise-wide networks as well as software migration and Reengineering intelligence programs.

Verity
Headquarters
1550 Plymouth Street
Mountain View, CA 94043
http://www.verity.com

Other Addresses:

1420 Spring Hill Road, McLean, VA 22103

Verity Inc. develops and markets information agent products and technologies that make it easier for individuals, workgroups, departments and enterprises to filter, search, retrieve, analyze and navigate all available information sources to get the personalized, relevant information they need. Customers include the Defense Intelligence Agency.

Vredenburg Corporation
1835 Alexander Bell Drive
Reston, VA
http://www.Vrendenburg.com

Other Addresses:

2341 Jefferson Davis Highway, Arlington, VA

Wang Laboratories, Inc.
Headquarters
600 Technology Park
Dr. Billerica, MA 01821-4130

Other Addresses:

Wang Federal Systems, Inc., 7900 Westpark Drive, McLean, VA
22102

Wang Laboratories, Inc. has 5,900 employees and annual sales of $946
million. The Wang Federal Systems Inc. subsidiary, with 1,100 employees, is a leading supplier of information technology systems and services
to the US Federal Government and government contractors. Wang
Federal Systems combines the resources of Wang's former Federal
Systems Division and HFSI (formerly Honeywell Federal Systems), the
worldwide systems integrator acquired early in 1995. As a major
integrator, HFSI has over 25 years of successful experience with the
Federal Government that includes the management of major DoD
programs such as the World-Wide Military Command and Control
System (WWMCCS) and Shipboard Non-tactical ADP Programs
(SNAP). With the HFSI acquisition, Wang Federal is the contractor for
the government's largest database contract (HFSI Database Machine
Contract), offering a client/server solution consisting of a Sybase system
running on Sun SPARC Server 2000s.

Now known as the Database Machine (DBM) contract this
Government-Wide Agency Contract [GWAC] is usable by all US
Government DOD and Civilian Agencies, and is"owned" by the Army,
Navy, Air Force, Defense Logistics Agency, Defense Information
Systems Agency, and the Internal Revenue Service. The Sybase System
10 Client/Server Architecture is the centerpiece of the HFSI Database
Machine Contract. HFSI is providing Sun's newest and fastest enterprise-

level server, the SPARCcenter 2000, as the Database Machine platform. With nearly 700 GB of directly connected disk storage, the architecture supports addition of RAID devices, jukeboxes, and tape silos.

Watkins-Johnson Company
3333 Hillview Ave.
Palo Alto, CA 93404

Other Addresses:

700 Quince Orchard Road, Gaithersburg, MD 20878

With $285 million in annual sales, this company provides semiconductor manufacturing equipment, military signals intelligence equipment and environmental consulting services.

Wheat International Communications
8229 Boone Blvd.
Vienna, VA 22182

Wheat International, with $3 million in annual sales, provides information technology engineering services, including communications network planning, design and project management (10)

The Author

MARK W. MERRITT belongs to a very special club whose members love working in secret operations. Involved in the field of special operations for more than 15 years, Mark as worked with the Joint Special Operations, intelligence, and counterintelligence communities as well as operations with the US Army. He is skilled in counterintelligence; intelligence collection, analysis and dissemination; mission planning; covered programs; intelligence photography; data communications and intelligence software systems and applications.

Since leaving the military, Mark has worked for three civilian employers: ORION Scientific, Inc, an international consulting firm which designs special operations/low-intensity conflict research and automated support for clients such as Defense Intelligence Agency, State Department, CIA, Department of Energy, Secret Service, International Association of Chiefs of Police and all branches of the Department of Defense; Sterling Software, Inc. where he provided analytical support, training, and training documentation to the Defense Intelligence Threat Data System and served as a "Tactical Asset" to theater commanders when deployed to hostile and semi-hostile environments to support utilization and training of the TRRIP system in Croatia, Turkey, and the European theater; and TRW where he provides Open Source Intelligence support as a Senior Information Officer for the Analysis and Study Group.

A graduate of the State University of New York (B.A., History) and St. Lawrence University (M.A., Counseling and Human Development), Mark is a member of several professional intelligence associations and holds a second degree Black Belt in Korean Tae Kwon Do. He is an avid mountaineer, kayaker, skier, archer, scuba diver, and holds an international pilots license for paragliding.

Career Resources

C ontact Impact Publications for an annotated listing of career resources by visiting their "Military Career Transition Center" and "Career Superstore and Warehouse" on the World Wide Web: *http://www.impactpublications.com*

The following career resources,are available directly from Impact Publications. Complete the following form or list the titles, include postage (see formula at the end), enclose payment, and send to:

IMPACT PUBLICATIONS
9104-N Manassas Drive
Manassas Park, VA 20111-5211
Tel. 703/361-7300 or Fax 703/335-9486
E-mail address: impactp@impactpublications.com

Orders from individuals must be prepaid by check, moneyorder, Visa, MasterCard, or American Express. We accept telephone and fax orders.

Qty.	TITLES	Price	TOTAL
___	Alternative Careers in Secret Operations	$19.95	_____
___	Classified Top Secret CD-ROM: The Definitive Word on the Cold War	49.95	_____

Military

Qty.	TITLES	Price	TOTAL
___	Becoming a Better Leader and Getting Promoted in Today's Army	13.95	_____
___	Beyond the Uniform	14.95	_____
___	Complete Guide to the NCO-ER	13.95	_____

___	**CORPORATE GRAY SERIES**	**51.95** ___
___	▪ From Air Force Blue to Corporate Gray	17.95 ___
___	▪ From Army Green to Corporate Gray	17.95 ___
___	▪ From Navy Blue to Corporate Gray	17.95 ___
___	Job Search: Marketing Your Military Experience	16.95 ___
___	Jobs and the Military Spouse	14.95 ___
___	New Relocating Spouse's Guide/Employment	14.95 ___
___	Out of Uniform	12.95 ___
___	Retiring From the Military	25.95 ___
___	Resumes and Job Search Letters for Transitioning Military Personnel	17.95 ___
___	Today's Military Wife	16.95 ___
___	Up or Out: How to Get Promoted/Army Draws Down	13.95 ___

Key Directories/Reference Works

___	American Almanac of Jobs and Salaries	20.00 ___
___	American Salaries & Wages Survey	105.00 ___
___	Big Book of Minority Opportunities	39.95 ___
___	Business Phone Book USA 1998	135.00 ___
___	Dictionary of Occupational Titles	39.95 ___
___	Directory of Executive Recruiters 1998	44.95 ___
___	Directory of Federal Jobs and Employers	21.95 ___
___	Government Phone Book USA 1998	185.00 ___
___	**JOB FINDERS FOR 1997-1998**	**50.95** ___
___	▪ Government Job Finder	16.95 ___
___	▪ Nonprofit's and Education Job Finder	16.95 ___
___	▪ Professional's Job Finder	18.95 ___
___	Job Hunter's Sourcebook	70.00 ___
___	Jobs Rated Almanac	16.95 ___
___	Moving & Relocation Sourcebook	179.95 ___
___	National Trade & Professional Associations	85.00 ___
___	Occupational Outlook Handbook	16.95 ___
___	Professional Careers Sourcebook	99.00 ___
___	Vocational Careers Sourcebook	82.00 ___

City and State Job Banks

___	**METROPOLITAN EMPLOYER CONTACT DIRECTORIES KIT** (37 titles)	**619.95** ___
___	▪ Atlanta (Job Bank)	16.95 ___
___	▪ Atlanta (How to Get a Job in)	16.95 ___
___	▪ Austin/San Antonio (Job Bank)	16.95 ___
___	▪ Boston (Job Bank)	16.95 ___
___	▪ Carolina (Job Bank)	15.95 ___
___	▪ Cincinnati (Job Bank)	16.95 ___
___	▪ Chicago (Job Bank)	16.95 ___
___	▪ Chicago (How to Get a Job in)	16.95 ___
___	▪ Cleveland (Job Bank)	16.95 ___
___	▪ Dallas/Fort Worth (Job Bank)	16.95 ___
___	▪ Denver (Job Bank)	15.95 ___

____	▪ Detroit (Job Bank)	16.95 ____
____	▪ Florida (Job Bank)	16.95 ____
____	▪ Houston (Job Bank)	16.95 ____
____	▪ Indianapolis (Job Bank)	16.95 ____
____	▪ Las Vegas (Job Bank)	16.95 ____
____	▪ Los Angeles (Job Bank)	16.95 ____
____	▪ Minneapolis/St. Paul (Job Bank)	16.95 ____
____	▪ Missouri (Job Bank)	16.95 ____
____	▪ New Mexico (Job Bank)	16.95 ____
____	▪ New York (Job Bank)	16.95 ____
____	▪ New York (How to Get a Job in)	16.95 ____
____	▪ North New England (Job Bank)	16.95 ____
____	▪ Ohio (Job Bank)	16.95 ____
____	▪ Philadelphia (Job Bank)	16.95 ____
____	▪ Phoenix (Job Bank)	15.95 ____
____	▪ Pittsburgh (Job Bank)	16.95 ____
____	▪ Portland (Job Bank)	16.95 ____
____	▪ San Francisco (Job Bank)	16.95 ____
____	▪ San Francisco (How to Get a Job in)	16.95 ____
____	▪ Seattle (Job Bank)	16.95 ____
____	▪ Seattle/Portland (How to Get a Job in)	16.95 ____
____	▪ Southern California (How to Get a Job in)	16.95 ____
____	▪ Tennessee (Job Bank)	16.95 ____
____	▪ Upstate New York (Job Bank)	16.95 ____
____	▪ Virginia (Job Bank)	16.95 ____
____	▪ Washington, DC (Job Bank)	16.95 ____

Using the Internet and Computers

____	Electronic Resumes For the New Job Market	11.95 ____
____	Finding a Job On the Internet	16.95 ____
____	How to Get Your Dream Job Using the Web	29.99 ____
____	Using the Internet and the WWW in Your Job Search	16.95 ____

Finding Great Jobs and Careers

____	Best Jobs For the 21st Century	19.95 ____
____	Careers in High Tech	17.95 ____
____	Change Your Job, Change Your Life	17.95 ____
____	Complete Idiot's Guide to Getting the Job You Want	24.95 ____
____	Directory of Executive Recruiters 1997	44.95 ____
____	Five Secrets to Finding a Job	12.95 ____
____	How to Get Interviews From Classified Job Ads	14.95 ____
____	How to Succeed Without a Career Path	13.95 ____
____	In Transition	12.50 ____
____	Job Hunting For Dummies	16.99 ____
____	Jobs 1998	15.00 ____
____	Jobs and Careers With Nonprofit Organizations	15.95 ____
____	Jobs For Lawyers	14.95 ____
____	Joyce Lain Kennedy's Career Book	29.95 ____
____	Knock 'Em Dead 1998	12.95 ____

____ New Rites of Passage at $100,000+	29.95	____
____ What Color Is Your Parachute? 1998	16.95	____

Cover Letters

____ 201 Dynamite Job Search Letters	19.95	____
____ 201 Killer Cover Letters	16.95	____
____ 201 Winning Cover Letters for $100,000+ Jobs	24.95	____
____ Cover Letters For Dummies	12.99	____
____ Dynamite Cover Letters	14.95	____

Resumes

____ 100 Winning Résumés for $100,000+ Jobs	24.95	____
____ 175 High-Impact Résumés	10.95	____
____ 1500+ KeyWords for $100,000+ Jobs	14.95	____
____ Asher's Bible of Executive Résumés	29.95	____
____ Best Résumés for $75,000+ Executive Jobs	18.95	____
____ Complete Idiot's Guide to Crafting the Perfect Résumé	16.95	____
____ Dynamite Résumés	14.95	____
____ High Impact Résumés and Letters	19.95	____
____ Résumé Catalog	15.95	____
____ Résumé Shortcuts	14.95	____
____ Résumés for Ex-Military Personnel	9.95	____
____ Résumés That Knock 'Em Dead	10.95	____

Skills, Testing, Self-Assessment, Empowerment

____ 7 Habits of Highly Effective People	14.00	____
____ Discover the Best Jobs for You	14.95	____
____ Do What You Are	16.95	____
____ Do What You Love, the Money Will Follow	10.95	____

Dress and Etiquette

____ Executive Etiquette in the New Workplace	14.95	____
____ John Molloy's New Dress For Success (Men)	13.99	____
____ *New* Women's Dress For Success	12.99	____
____ Red Socks Don't Work!	14.95	____
____ Winning Image	17.95	____

Networking and Power Building

____ Dynamite Networking For Dynamite Jobs	15.95	____
____ Dynamite Tele-Search	12.95	____
____ Great Connections	19.95	____
____ How to Work a Room	11.99	____
____ Power Schmoozing	12.95	____
____ Power to Get In	24.95	____
____ Secrets of Savvy Networking	12.99	____

Interviewing

___	101 Dynamite Answers to Interview Questions	12.95 ___
___	101 Dynamite Questions to Ask at Your Job Interview	14.95 ___
___	101 Great Answers/Interview Questions	9.99 ___
___	111 Dynamite Ways to Ace Your Job Interview	13.95 ___
___	Dynamite Salary Negotiations	15.95 ___
___	Interview For Success	15.95 ___
___	Job Interviews For Dummies	12.99 ___
___	Killer Interviews	10.95 ___
___	Naked At the Interview	10.95 ___
___	NBEW's Interviewing	11.95 ___

SUBTOTAL ___

Virginia residents add 4½% sales tax ___

SHIPPING/HANDLING ($5.00 for first $5.00
title plus 8% of SUBTOTAL over $30) ___

TOTAL ENCLOSED -------------------- ___

SHIP TO:

NAME _____

ADDRESS _____

_____

❑ I enclose check/moneyorder for $ _____ made payable to
IMPACT PUBLICATIONS.

❑ Please charge $ _____ to my credit card:

❑ Visa   ❑ MasterCard   ❑ American Express

Card # _____

Expiration date: _____/_____

Signature _____

We accept official purchase orders from libraries, educational institutions, and
government offices. Please attach copy with official signature(s).

The On-Line Superstore & Warehouse

Hundreds of Terrific Career Resources Conveniently Available On the World Wide Web 24-Hours a Day, 365 Days a Year!

Ever wanted to know what are the newest and best books, directories, newsletters, wall charts, training programs, videos, CD-ROMs, computer software, and kits available to help you land a job, negotiate a higher salary, or start your own business? What about finding a job in Asia or relocating to San Francisco? Are you curious about how to find a job 24-hours a day by using the Internet or what you'll be doing five years from now? Trying to keep up-to-date on the latest career resources but not able to find the latest catalogs, brochures, or newsletters on today's "best of the best" resources?

Welcome to the first virtual career bookstore on the Internet. Now you're only a "click" away with Impact Publication's electronic solution to the resource challenge. Impact Publications, one of the nation's leading publishers and distributors of career resources, has launched its comprehensive "Career Superstore and Warehouse" on the Internet. The bookstore is jam-packed with the latest job and career resources on:

- Alternative jobs and careers
- Self-assessment
- Career planning and job search
- Employers
- Relocation and cities
- Resumes
- Cover Letters
- Dress, image, and etiquette
- Education
- Telephone
- Military
- Salaries
- Interviewing
- Nonprofits

- Empowerment
- Self-esteem
- Goal setting
- Executive recruiters
- Entrepreneurship
- Government
- Networking
- Electronic job search
- International jobs
- Travel
- Law
- Training and presentations
- Minorities
- Physically challenged

The bookstore also includes a new "Military Career Transition Center" and "School-to-Work Center."

"This is more than just a bookstore offering lots of product," say Drs. Ron and Caryl Krannich, two of the nation's leading career experts and authors and developers of this on-line bookstore. *"We're an important resource center for libraries, corporations, government, educators, trainers, and career counselors who are constantly defining and redefining this dynamic field. Of the thousands of career resources we review each year, we only select the 'best of the best.'"*

Visit this rich site and you'll quickly discover just about everything you ever wanted to know about finding jobs, changing careers, and starting your own business—including many useful resources that are difficult to find in local bookstores and libraries. The site also includes what's new and hot, tips for job search success, and monthly specials. Impact's Web address is:

http://www.impactpublications.com